I read this amazing book w
with terminal cancer. It is a t.
practical road map, to help and support not only the person
who is dying, but those who love and are caring for that person.
There were lots of things we were able to do to make the most
of our time together, all suggested by this wonderful resource.
Thank you for a book that deals head on with the things we are
so often afraid to talk or think about, and thank you for helping
us navigate this part of our friendship.

Liz Smith, lawyer, Vancouver, Canada

Beautifully put and tremendously approachable; I am so glad
someone has written such an approachable book that gently
and tenderly discusses this critically important topic. I found
the book quite uplifting despite the seriousness of the subject
and plan to recommend it to many of my patients.

Dr JF MD, Palliative Psychiatry, New York, USA

This book should be required reading for everybody. Both
inspirational and thought-provoking, it deals with the situations
and emotions that we felt when our lives were touched by the
recent, untimely death of a loved one. We coped by blindly
stumbling our way through, but the practical and honest way
that the advice in this book is presented, would have made
their end of life and the continuing lives of those of us
surrounding, so much more bearable if we'd been able to learn
from it, at that terrible time. We cannot recommend it highly
enough.

Matthew and Louise Charlesworth, Bournemouth, England

An important guide to a journey we will all have to make.

Bruno Huber, British Columbia, Mexico & the Caribbean

Lap of Honour

A no fear guide
to living well with dying

Gaby Eirew and Dr Pippa Hawley

FIRST EDITION
ISBN   978-1-7751811-0-1 (paperback)

Publishers: Gaby Eirew and Dr Pippa Hawley
Cover design: Andrej Semnic, aka Semnitz
Typeset by Ken Boyter

Photographs by Bill Hawley (www.billhawleyphotography.com) unless otherwise stated.

Quotation in Chapter 8 from *Final Journeys: A Practical Guide for Bringing Care and Comfort at the End of Life* by Maggie Callanan (Penguin Random House 2009).

Thank you to Northern Health for permission to reproduce their MOST form in Chapter 5.

Disclaimer
All opinions presented are those of the authors. Neither author represents any organization in the writing of this book. All Individuals and scenarios mentioned are included either with permission from those involved, or where this was not possible, any potentially identifying information has been changed to protect the confidentiality of those concerned. This book is intended to provide general information and not intended as medical advice; if you have specific medical questions you should seek counsel from a medical or counselling professional. Similarly, if you have financial, psychological or social questions, you should seek counsel from a relevant professional.

Pippa's acknowledgements

Thanks to Bill for taking all the lovely photos (www.billhawleyphotography.com), and to Roger, Andrew Mason, Lib Cooper and Cindy Lou, Sue Wong and her patient grandchildren for being willing to be photographed. To Sharie and Chris for sharing their photos and memories. Thanks also to LuAnne Morrow, Oleh Ilnyckyj and Bill McNaughton. Thanks to my colleagues at BC Cancer and the UBC Division of Palliative Care, especially Kathryn Inman and Charlie Chen, for being a constant source of inspiration and support.

Thanks most of all to my patients, who have taught me pretty much all I know. Some extra-special people come to mind, including Mark Roberts, Euan Lynch, Mary Beckwith (Nyland), Timm Morrow, Rob Pollock, Kenny Do, Ian Reid, Ken Swenerton, Patricia Greenwood and John Barrett. Their legacy, and that of many more, lives on.

Gaby's acknowledgements

I am so delighted this book is here. Thanks go to the many institutions that worked with us and to the Hormbrey family and Denise Shenton who first inspired my learning. Thanks to Recordmenow for permission to use our research and app, and to Board members, lawyer James Leong, physician Dr Quynh Doan, teacher Allie Bird, and hospice founder Sue Wong, for your wisdom. Love and thanks to Dr Peter Eirew, CL Lynch, Sydney Foran, Inbar Shai, Dr James Fraiman, Scott Jones, Leslie Fulton, Suzanne Hindley and Mandy Tanner for all your great work and jolly support, and to the Persula Foundation for your philanthropic kindness. Kate Miller committed, supported, encouraged and edited us wonderfully. Carol coached us gently, Ken Boyter designed and laid out the book and Semnitz designed the cover. Pepi, Milo, David and Peter walked the dog, made so many dinners and waited patiently. A community of people contributed to this book. I miss and always will be grateful to my dad Ernest Shenton, my mother in law Dr Roz Eirew, and friends Sue Harris and David Brown, who graciously shared what it means to live well with dying.

www.lapofhonourbook.com

Dedicated to:

Dr Edward Adib Massey who knew how to live real life well; bright lovelies Peter, Milo, David and Pepi; and reader, for you, for comfort, connection and making good memories.

Gaby Eirew

Nick, Fred and Bill, my ever-tolerant men, and to Ben, who sadly didn't have enough time for any of this.

Dr Pippa Hawley

Introduction

Thank you for at least getting this far! Just so you know what you are getting into, this book is intended to offer practical help when you are learning to live with a potentially life-threatening illness. It is also intended to be of use to the family and caregivers of people in that situation. Despite the challenges ahead, we want you all to have as much fun and as few regrets as possible.

The advice offered here is based on the experiences of many people whom we have had the privilege to get to know, and also of those who treated and cared for them. Where there is relevant research it is evidence-based, but in large part it is 'experience-based'. As authors, we bring together our different skills and experience of working with people in all stages of illness. Between us, we look at the range of issues facing you as you enter the final lap of your life's course.

All of us will one day find that our life has run its course. Some runners stop at the finish line. Others take their time, grab a flag, cheer with the crowd and feel the love back. They do a lap of honour, recognizing everything that brought them to this moment, all the events in their life and all the people who are key to them.

Whatever your state of health, it is always possible to live your life and enjoy your lap of honour, and this book sets out to help you do that.

So how did we come to write this book?

Back in 2011, we realized that though there are many books addressing people's emotional and spiritual needs when they are ill, and some excellent disease-specific patient guides (mainly for cancer), there is very little out there for people who just want practical advice to help them carry on with their lives, choosing to do the best they can with whatever health and whatever time they have. The Recordmenow helpline and app, set up by Gaby to assist people in leaving a message-legacy for their loved ones, were getting many requests for support with end-of-life issues, and people who had attended Pippa's Bucket List Festivals were asking for a similar resource in book form.

Between us, we have many years' experience in hospitals, clinics and hospices, and our perspectives are complementary. As a team, we hope that we have provided the practical tips people were asking for.

When you have been diagnosed with an illness (or someone close to you has) you enter a rather unusual time. Life's finishing line might be drawing nearer, but you are still very much alive. This is a time of huge opportunity for warmth, connection and honesty. There are unknowns and inevitably there will be fears, yet once you have a sense of what to expect, fears can be much more manageable, and the personal growth often described by people in this situation can be maximized. There may be difficult conversations ahead, but if these are tackled with honesty and kindness, they can be uplifting.

Almost everything discussed in this book is appropriate whatever illness you have, almost wherever you are. The most common long-term diseases which people in the developed world live with are cancer, heart disease, chronic lung disease, kidney failure, stroke and dementia, but the list is long. What people have in common is that they want to live as well as possible, for as long as possible. This may sound obvious, but it's actually not that easy to do. There are some things you need to know to be able to do this. We will try to cover as many of them as possible. Use this book like a salad bar and pick and choose different sections. You don't have to read them in order, and you might not feel ready to tackle some initially, but then you can come back to them if you wish. If you think of anything important which we have missed out, let us know and we'll include it in our next edition.

> *Advice for people who just want to carry on with their lives, choosing to do the best they can with what health they have*

Modern medicine has changed the way serious illnesses progress. In past centuries most people died quickly, at home or at work, after accidents or from infectious illnesses such as pneumonia, tuberculosis, or epidemics like influenza or smallpox. Over the years our lifestyles have changed, our health has improved, and we now live longer than ever in history. Among significant-sized countries in the world, in the top five for life expectancy – Japan, Singapore, Switzerland, Australia and Spain – men live to just over 80 years, and women to about 85. In most countries, women in general live about five years longer than men.

In the countries at the bottom of this list, the average life lasts 50 years. But this average includes all the people who don't make it to adulthood, and those who die young of AIDS or war. Even in those countries, there are people who dodge their way through childhood, and then go on to live to a ripe old age. So, no matter what statistics say, there are always people who defy expectations and end up with very different outcomes to those predicted.

Rapid developments (for example in cancer drugs) mean it is very difficult now for doctors to say with any certainty what lies ahead for people who have received a diagnosis of life-threatening illness. Not knowing which day will be your last can be very scary, but it can also be liberating. If you have the goal of going to bed every night feeling that it would be OK if that day ended up being your last, you would spend less time doing meaningless or tiresome things.

It can, however, be hard to get that happy medium. If you make grandiose plans for a long way ahead and then are too sick to actually enjoy them, you will have wasted a lot of money and set yourself up for disappointment. On the other hand, if you don't at least try, then you might eventually die of boredom! The people who have the most fun throughout their lives seem always to have set up something to look forward to. Yet they are also sensible about being prepared; staying flexible and willing to change the plan if circumstances alter.

Balance is the key to living well: making sure that you work enough to have a roof over your head and enough to eat; investing time in your loved ones so that you have company and people who care about you; having time to play, and time to explore your passions. When medical problems stop you from doing the things you want, there may be ways of adapting, so that you are still able to achieve your goals, or you may realize that your goals have changed. The philosophy of planning for the worst and hoping for the best is a pragmatic and constructive way of getting the most out of every day.

> *Planning for the worst and hoping for the best is a pragmatic and constructive way of getting the most out of every day*

The way we die is as important and as unique as each of us. This book is intended to give you the tools to work out what is best for you. We want this book to help you realize your hopes for the best, whilst enabling you to plan for the rest – so that you don't have to waste precious time worrying about it.

With ideas and information here that work in practice, this book means you don't have to do the legwork. It also means you can have a good reference wherever you are, to access in your own time, at your own pace. We also have a dynamic webpage – *www.lapofhonourbook.com* – which you can explore for more ideas and feedback about helpful facilities in your region.

In this book, we have no emotional, political, religious or denominational agenda whatsoever. We just want to offer something that helps you to live your life to the very end, enjoying your lap of honour, in the way that feels right for you.

Pippa and Gaby

Dr Pippa Hawley

Dr Pippa Hawley FRCPC (Pall Med) founded the supportive and palliative care service at British Columbia's cancer program in 1997 and remains its medical director. She is also a clinical professor and head of the Division of Palliative Care at the University of British Columbia. Pippa has a busy clinical, research and teaching practice, and designed the innovative 'Bowtie Model' of integrated palliative care in 2014 in an effort to break down the misperception that palliative care is only for people in the last few weeks of life. This has been adopted throughout the world, such that her name is recognizable to many professionals in palliative and hospice care worldwide.

Gaby Eirew

Gaby Eirew is a counsellor and educator and a recognized expert in what key messages parents should leave for their children. Gaby has directed two charities, been on the board of a hospice and presented a weekly hospital radio show. Gaby has been awarded Outstanding Philanthropist, Charity of the Year and Women of the Year commendations. She created Recordmenow, a free app which uses question-prompting to help people make video recordings to leave messages for their loved ones; this app has now helped tens of thousands of people in over 32 countries. Gaby trains medical students in learning about the importance of legacy, and lectures worldwide on 'dying well – the way you want'.

Chapter 1

How long have I got?
Diagnosis and prognostication

Dr Pippa Hawley

When we get to the end of our lives, most of us will know we are going to die, because we have been diagnosed with a disease which we know is not curable.

This simple statement however represents the state of understanding and acceptance which is the end point of a process. This process may be long or short, easy or hard, straightforward or convoluted, but usually looks something like this.

Healthy person ⇨ Something wrong ⇨Telling a doctor ⇨ List of possibilities ⇨ Tests ⇨ Results ⇨ Diagnosis ⇨ Sick person ⇨ Learning what to expect ⇨ Trying to fix it ⇨ Realization that it is not fixable ⇨ Acceptance of mortality

In her famous book *On Death and Dying* published in 1969, Elizabeth Kubler-Ross described a series of emotional states that people might go through during this process.

These 'Five stages of grief' were:

1) Denial

2) Anger

3) Bargaining

4) Depression

5) Acceptance.

Her description of the process was based on extensive experience as a psychiatrist working with people who had advanced incurable illnesses. Many of you reading this will be somewhere on the process above, and some of you will have experienced at least one or two of the five stages of grief (which, by the way, don't always occur).

Each step in the process, either situational or emotional, represents a transition, and each transition is an event which – though it may be traumatic – is an important positive step in getting closer to acceptance and getting on with making sure your bucket is full by the time you die.

In order to understand these steps, we will start with how a diagnosis is made, and then describe how doctors try to predict what will happen: a process known as prognostication.

Making a Diagnosis
Symptoms

Any deviation from someone's normal feeling is called a symptom. Common symptoms include such unpleasant experiences as pain, shortness of breath, loss of appetite, nausea, vomiting, diarrhea, tiredness, itching and many others. The point at which a symptom might trigger a person to seek medical attention varies a lot from one person to the next. Some of us are hyper-vigilant and worry a lot about even minor changes from normal, and other people either don't really notice until a symptom is severe, or may be frightened to admit that there is anything wrong, in case it might be bad news.

It is important to get the balance right in deciding when to go to the doctor. If you go frequently, for minor ailments like colds and muscle sprains, you will waste a lot of time and may end up taking treatments that are actually unnecessary, potentially even harmful. An example of this is that antibiotics are of no value in treating viral infections, and can cause bacteria to become resistant to antibiotics, so that when you have a real bacterial infection, the drugs don't work.

On the other hand, you don't want to leave a symptom, which could be caused by a disease which may be curable if caught early, such as cancer. Many cancers can now be cured if they are detected before they have grown too big to remove, or spread to other parts of the body. With a few exceptions, in general when a cancer has spread through the bloodstream to another part, such as the liver (metastasized), it is not curable. Exceptions to this include testicular cancer (as demonstrated by Lance Armstrong) and cancers of the lymph system (lymphomas) or blood (leukemias). These are the main kinds of cancer which often can be cured, despite having spread throughout the body.

The outcomes for heart problems too are so much better if diagnosed early. Chest pain on exertion may be caused by narrowing of the arteries to the heart muscle and, if left untreated, may progress to a heart attack, permanently damaging the heart muscle and potentially later on leading to heart failure. But if treated promptly when chest pain is first felt, damage to the heart can be forestalled, and the arteries opened up to prevent future damage.

When you go to see your doctor, they will ask you about your symptoms, and some of their questions may not initially make sense. Be patient and complete in your responses, as the doctor is trying to identify a pattern which might enable them to figure out what is wrong.

A good example of a symptom which could signify many different illnesses is back pain. Simultaneous yellowing of the eyes, pale floaty bowel movements and itching point strongly to cancer of the pancreas. On the other hand, the vast majority of people have had back pain at some time in their life, and very, very few of them have pancreatic cancer. Most of them have mild arthritis of the spine, are overweight or don't get enough exercise, or have pulled a muscle by lifting something badly. By asking questions about exactly where the pain is, what it feels like, when it started, what makes it better or worse, and about any other symptoms which may be associated with the pain, the doctor can identify details which are important in establishing the most likely cause. Physical examination may help in refining the list of possibilities further.

Tests and screening

Sometimes the pattern of symptoms and examination findings are so suggestive of one single problem that the diagnosis may be very obvious, but often it is only possible to come up with a short list, which requires further investigation. This is called a differential diagnosis. Medical tests are then ordered and the results used to whittle down the possibilities, ideally until there is only one diagnosis left.

In reality, however, most medical tests are not perfect. Some tests are very sensitive, in that they are nearly always positive in the condition being looked for, for example testing for blood in faeces for bowel cancer, but they can also be not very specific, in that the test can also show positive for lots of people in whom there isn't anything wrong. These tests can sometimes be unhelpful if they create anxiety about the possibility of having something seriously wrong when in fact you are perfectly healthy.

The decision as to whether or not to do a test can be quite tricky, and large studies involving thousands of people are sometimes necessary to help decide on the value of an individual test, especially in the absence of symptoms.

Some tests done as screening i.e. in people who have no symptoms, are controversial. They can actually cause more harm than good, if more people are harmed by the interventions resulting from a positive test than are helped because the test reveals the presence of the disease. Mammography for breast cancer, and the prostate specific antigen (PSA) blood test for prostate cancer are good examples of screening tests where the benefits and the risks are very closely balanced. There are good arguments for only doing them in people who have a risk factor which makes them more likely than most to have the disease, such as having close family members that have already had it. Colonoscopy is another example of a test which can cause harm (and also be extremely unpleasant) but can be life-saving if it picks up a cancer when it is early and curable.

Other tests can be quite specific, in that if they are negative it is very unlikely that you have the disease being tested for, but not very sensitive, in that they can fail to show positive in people who do actually have the disease. These tests can be very useful in excluding certain diseases. For example, the negative blood test for hepatitis B very conclusively rules out infection with that particular virus.

The reality of tests is that very few of them have the perfect attributes of being highly sensitive and highly specific, so doctors sometimes have to use a combination of tests to be sure. Sometimes they also need to repeat tests after a while, as changes may take time to appear. An example of this is when someone has a dizzy spell, and some difficulty speaking or moving an arm. A CT scan of the head may be normal when done during a visit to the hospital emergency department, but one taken a week later may show signs of the stroke which caused the symptoms.

Breaking bad news

Once your doctor has figured out what is the most likely diagnosis, he or she will try to tell you, preferably in person. A humane way of breaking bad news has been taught to medical students and young doctors for some years now, but not all doctors have received this training, especially older ones, and like all learned skills, some are better at it than others.

If you have been asked to meet with your doctor to discuss the results of some tests, it is possible that bad news may need to be broken and it is a good idea for you to be prepared. Just as the doctor should make appropriate preparations, like allowing sufficient time, making sure they won't be interrupted, and having all the information available, so also should you prepare.

How to be prepared for hearing the results

Bring a trusted companion with you. If it's good news you can celebrate together afterwards! If it does turn out to be bad news, you have someone to drive you home, explain to other family members what is wrong and make sure you are well looked after.

Be ready to make notes. Some people also like to record the conversation, so that they can listen to it again together later. People generally only recall about a third of the information they are told in an appointment with a doctor and it is very common for people to stop absorbing information after the initial shock of being told something bad, for example that you have heart failure or cancer. The important subsequent details, such as how advanced it is and what treatments are available, may not register at all in your memory. Having this information written down, recorded, or remembered by your companion can be very useful once you have got over the initial shock and need to plan for what's ahead.

Treatments and outcomes

When a diagnosis of a life-threatening illness is made, people's first concern is usually to know what to expect, both in terms of possible treatments, and possible outcomes.

Often it is hard to be sure of likely outcomes until some time has passed, and the responsiveness of the disease to various treatments has been tested. As time goes by it becomes clearer as to how things are going to go. For example, some cancers can be cured by early surgery, especially with additional radiotherapy and/or chemotherapy, but despite the best of surgical techniques and the most sophisticated tests currently available, no-one knows right away if a few cancer cells have been left behind or not. These cells can sit in your liver or bone marrow sometimes for years, waiting for some unpredictable moment to start causing trouble again. This is called 'recurrence'.

In order to maximize the chance of a cure, the doctors give you the strongest additional or 'adjuvant' treatment they feel you can tolerate in the hope of killing every last cancer cell, but in truth no-one really knows who needs the stronger treatments, and who will not be cured. Some will have awful side-effects from the treatments that may actually have been unnecessary, and some may get recurrent disease despite receiving the strongest treatments. The problem is, we can't currently predict whose cancer will come back and whose won't.

Oncologists do their best to predict who will respond best to treatment based on a variety of factors, and then current best practice is to give everyone with the same kind of cancer much the same treatment. This however is changing. Discovery of characteristics which can help discriminate better between cancers have allowed for dramatic advances in cancer treatments. For example, many cancers are now tested not just for what cell type they have and how far through the body they have spread, but also whether the cells show receptors for certain proteins on their surfaces. Being positive for these receptors makes these cells more likely to respond to certain drugs. This 'personalized medicine' is an area of very active medical research. Similarly, advances are regularly being made in other serious illnesses that can dramatically change outcomes, especially in organ transplantation and procedures for heart disease such as valve replacement. For example, procedures that used to require major surgery requiring weeks of recovery can now be done in some centres with patients discharged home only a day or two later.

Prognostication

Once a person's illness becomes very advanced, doctors may be able to say with reasonable accuracy how long the person is expected to live, but in general no doctor's estimate of life expectancy is better than a guess. Doctors have been consistently shown to over-estimate life expectancy, but those with the most experience tend to make the most accurate guesses. Interestingly, the guesses get worse the better the doctor knows the patient, as emotional attachment gets in the way of logic. The guesses do tend to get more accurate the sicker the patient gets. This process of trying to predict life expectancy is called prognostication, and is still considered an art acquired through years of experience.

Much work is being done to try to convert the art of prognostication into a science by studying what features are associated with poorer or better outcomes in various illnesses. Though some objective measures can be combined to make an index which is helpful, they always result in a range of possible times.

The important thing to remember is that a prognosis is only a best guess as to what will happen to an average person with your condition, and not to you personally. An average is the point at which half the people with what you have will do better, and half will do worse, sometimes much better or much worse.

So why bother with prognostication at all you might ask? A good question, and one which many people use to avoid the subject altogether. It can however be useful to have a rough idea of what to expect. There are sometimes very good reasons to have a prognosis. You might need to know before you plan a long holiday to somewhere with poor medical services. A son or daughter may like the option of bringing forward their wedding plans to be sure that you will be able to attend. A thriving small business could be sold with good value whilst still fully operational, allowing your family to benefit, instead of the business declining because you are not able to give it your full attention.

Sometimes the time and effort needed to participate in a clinical trial of a new treatment, or going to the hospital for time-consuming treatments, such as dialysis, may use up a large proportion of your time and prevent you from doing important things. Visiting relatives far away or spending time with your children might be a better use of your time instead of staying in a hotel next to a specialist treatment centre hundreds of miles away from your loved ones.

For these reasons, your doctor may ask if you would like them to offer a prognosis. If you say yes, please understand that your doctor is trying to give the best chance of making the most of your remaining life. A prognosis gives you the opportunity to get cracking with your bucket list. But also understand that likelihood of the time suggested being exactly correct is small, and don't get cross with your doctor should they be wrong!

Chapter 2

How can I face the unknown?
Dealing with the fear of dying

Dr Pippa Hawley

'Knowledge is the antidote to fear'
– Ralph Waldo Emerson

Most people do not actually fear being dead. They may be sad at losing future opportunities, and worry about what will happen to their loved ones left behind, but ceasing to physically exist is not inherently scary to most people. Many, however, are frightened of the process of actually getting there. As Woody Allen said: 'I am not afraid of death, I just don't want to be there when it happens.'

Being frightened of dying is not surprising given our exposure to death in modern times. Dying is almost always portrayed in the media as dramatic and unpleasant, usually as a result of violence, suffering, or extreme deprivation. Even if a character's life is portrayed as exceptionally hard, the alternative (death) is considered even less attractive. To quote Woody Allen again: 'Life is full of misery, loneliness, and suffering – and it's all over much too soon.'

Humour is definitely one of the ways in which human beings face down their fear of death. Bill Shankly, manager of the famous English soccer team Liverpool in the 1970s, was famous for his quip that people were wrong to believe that football is a matter of life and death – 'It is much, much more important than that.' After his team beat their arch-rivals (Everton) in the 1971 FA cup semi-final, he said: 'Sickness would not have kept me away from this one. If I'd been dead, I would have had them bring the casket to the ground, prop it up in the stands and cut a hole in the lid.'

Fear of the unknown

As no-one really knows what being dead feels like, fear of death represents fear of the unknown, especially as our opportunities to witness dying become fewer.

Dying used to be a family affair. The body was laid out, and the open coffin displayed on the dining room table for a few days. Then a great big party was held to say goodbye. Tears were shed, but there was also laughter and storytelling about the deceased. By exposure, natural dying becomes less terrifying because it is no longer unknown.

The days of seeing older relatives die in their own beds in your multigenerational home are, in many urban societies, long gone. In most developed countries, it is now more common to die in hospital or a nursing home than at home. All too often the actual moment of ceasing to live can go unwitnessed, as it happens during sleep, or when the nurse is seeing to other patients. Dying alone is probably not the best for the patient, but the survivors also suffer from missing the opportunity to be there in a person's last moments.

Diagnosis of dying
– an invaluable skill

When a death is anticipated, care can be focused on creating comfort and peace, but sometimes it is not clear that someone is actually dying until very near the end. There are a number of patients I remember quite vividly from my early months in practice: I wished I had recognized that their death was imminent, so that I had time to better prepare them and their families. This 'diagnosis of dying' is an important skill which has not traditionally been part of medical education, but was one of the most useful things I learned in my first job, in a small hospital in the south of England.

> **When a death is anticipated, care can be focused on creating comfort and peace**

I remember looking after a teenage boy with leukaemia, in the days before bone marrow transplants. Hematologists were becoming quite excited by a small number of drugs becoming available which seemed to be effective in killing cancerous cells in the bone marrow. The hospital was a small one, but very proud of its special barrier nursing room, where patients undergoing immunosuppressive chemotherapy could be protected from germs. There was a one-way pressurized airflow system, and visitors all had to wash their hands and wear gowns, masks and gloves to go in. It took a few minutes to get all this on before going into the room, and once on the outfit was awfully hot. In a busy day with lots of blood tests to draw, patients to be seen, notes to be written, and books to be studied, it was easy to put off visiting this young man because of the time it took to get washed and into the outfit.

This lovely boy spent weeks in that isolation room, with relatively infrequent visits. In the end, he deteriorated very quickly and his family was called in. There was a particularly good nurse in the room with him, wearing the isolation outfit, and she drew my attention through the window. He was losing consciousness rapidly and, realizing that there was nothing I could do to stop him dying, I went in right away in my ordinary clothes, hands unwashed. I held his hand and said goodbye, hoping that he was aware I was there, and that I was no longer looking like an alien. When his family arrived a few minutes later I could at least tell them that he didn't die in a totally sterile environment, and I hope that gave them some comfort later on, despite the awfulness of the situation.

This was an important learning experience for me, and I made sure it was not wasted. The next patients I looked after all benefited from my newly-recognized awareness of needing to be able to tell when someone was getting close to death. Over the years I think I have got better at this important skill, but it is not something which is easy to teach. For someone who has never before witnessed a death it can be impossible to recognize when it is close. The movies really aren't a reliable source of information here!

Illusions of immortality

The availability of amazing new treatments which can defy death creates the illusion that life can be prolonged indefinitely. If someone dies, the great medicines which have produced so many miracles in the last century and from which we all have such high expectations, are seen to have somehow failed.

Some people have gone to extraordinary lengths to try to deny their own mortality, to the point of being cryopreserved (frozen) with the expectation that at some time in the future it might be possible to thaw them out and enable them to be brought back to life. Institutions have been set up to research ways of prolonging life even further than we currently achieve, and the internet is festooned with dubious age-defying products, diets and theories. Unfortunately, though people are living longer overall, we will increasingly enter our final years with chronic illnesses.

The reality that we are all well aware of, even if we choose not to think about it for most of our lives, is that even the best modern medicines cannot keep anyone alive indefinitely.

Fighting a war

The less familiar we become with death, and the more powerful modern medicine seems to be, the scarier dying appears. The war metaphors that are so often used in reference to medical treatments compound this scaremongering. The well-known 'Ride to Conquer Cancer' is a good example, where thousands of people in matching shirts (like an army uniform) cycle for hours in the wind and rain, on a course which somehow seems to be uphill all the way, all in aid of raising money for cancer research. I have participated in the ride a number of times, and my research program would not exist without it. We are encouraged to feel like soldiers in a heroic battle. Our hearts are in our throats and our lower lips tremble with emotion as much as our legs tremble with fatigue as we cross the finish line, feeling like a gloriously victorious army.

Though with good intent, this is of course a ludicrous but deliberate manipulation of our emotions. Most of us are riding in memory of friends, parents, siblings, spouses or children we loved, but who died of cancer anyway, despite modern medicine's best efforts to delay their passing. By participating in these massive inspirational efforts, we are acknowledging our limitations, and our fear for our own futures. Through doing something in a big team we feel more powerful. But though clearly good comes from the effort in fundraising, the whole phenomenon of raising an army to fight cancer actually worsens the perception of the strength of the foe, thus strengthening 'the shadow'. Thinking of diseases such as cancer as powerful foes makes them more fearsome, and makes more people donate more money to try to beat them.

Religion and its role in coping

For centuries, religion has held all the cards in terms of shaping attitudes to death and dying, and this can have good and bad effects. Many people find strength in their faith in their god watching over and taking care of them. A belief in some sort of pleasant after-life can be very reassuring when facing death, even for people who are not religious. However, some people not only believe in hell but fear they will go there when they die; not surprisingly they have a really hard time when confronting their own mortality. This belief system is termed 'negative religious coping' and is often held by people who also believe that a higher power will punish them for their sins. These individuals may feel that their god has abandoned them when something bad happens. Fortunately, religious coping is more often positive than negative.

The Buddhist approach to dying is reassuringly clear that death is not the end of life, but rather the door that must be passed through to enter the next reincarnation. This reincarnation, or rebirth, does not involve the transference of an unchanging self or soul from one body to another. The form in which a body is reincarnated is affected by how the person behaved during their life, into a hierarchy of organisms depending on how 'good' the life was, referred to as 'karma'.

Islamic tradition is very specific as to what exactly happens before, during, and after death, similarly dependent on how the life had been lived. The Angel of Death (Malak al-Maut) comes to take the souls of the dying. Sinners' souls are extracted in a most painful way while the righteous are treated kindly. After the burial, two angels (Munkar and Nakir) arrive to question the dead to test their faith. The righteous believers are able to answer correctly and are allowed to live in the afterlife in peace and comfort, while the sinners and disbelievers can't answer the questions correctly and are duly punished for eternity.

The Jewish perspective is that we should always be mindful of our death, remembering to look after the welfare of the living – kavod he chai – and the respectful treatment of the dead – kavod ha-met. The focus is on preserving the dignity of the human spirit at all times.

In Judaism there is a belief in the afterlife. A body is not left unattended after death and burials happen within a few days wherever possible.

These are only a small selection of examples of cultural approaches to dying (many large books would be required to do this topic justice), but the bargaining concept that having been a good person will lead to a better afterlife appears consistently in religious teaching. Knowing what is 'good enough' might be a challenge.

All however is not lost: many cultures allow an escape clause, in that certain rituals are purported to offer absolution, making up for past misbehaviours. A Catholic apostolic pardon is a good example of a passive ritual. Some end-of-life bargaining rituals however involve suffering of some sort, the degree of suffering hopefully being sufficient to even out the sins.

Expectations from families and friends may differ from the actual person and can lead to conflict around interventions targeting relief of suffering.

Creating your own after-life

'The Soldier' by Rupert Brooke describes a young man's need to believe in an after-life when facing almost certain death in the First World War. Substituting patriotism for religion, he tackles his fear of the unknown by creating an imaginary heaven, made up from memories of his happiest times.

If I should die, think only this of me:
That there's some corner of a foreign field
That is for ever England. There shall be
In that rich earth a richer dust concealed;
A dust whom England bore, shaped, made aware,
Gave, once, her flowers to love, her ways to roam;
A body of England's, breathing English air,
Washed by the rivers, blest by suns of home.

And think, this heart, all evil shed away,
A pulse in the eternal mind, no less
Gives somewhere back the thoughts by England given;
Her sights and sounds; dreams happy as her day;
And laughter, learnt of friends; and gentleness,
In hearts at peace, under an English heaven.

Similarly, the poem 'I Am Not Gone', by Kenyan poet Injete Chesoni provides reassurance for those left behind, using 'blue sky' imagery.

I am not gone
I remain here beside you
Just in a different form
Look for me in your heart
And there you will find me
in our love which forever lives on
In those moments when you feel alone
Look for me in your thoughts
And there you will find me
in sweet memories that burn strong
Every time a tear
Forms in your beautiful eyes
Look up to the heavens
And there you will see me
Smiling down from God's glorious skies

So, when you are approaching your own death there are many ways of coping. Spirituality can provide a degree of strength and traditional rites can be comforting. However, in my observation traditional religion may not always be helpful, and can occasionally lead to more distress rather than less. Despite what some religious leaders may say, there are no set 'rules' on how to behave when approaching your death.

A strategy to face the fear

A good strategy is to remove as many unknowns as possible, so that whatever appears frightening is disempowered.

- Get as much information as possible about your condition and its possible complications.

- Establish a plan to deal with all predictable eventualities, and a few unlikely ones too, just to be on the safe side.

- Write it all down clearly and make sure it is accessible to people caring for you.

- Talk to your loved ones about what you believe happens after death.

> *Preparing to die needs work and planning if it is to be done well. Once this work is done, you can relax and enjoy the rest of your life*

Just as we go to ante-natal classes when expecting a baby, preparing to die needs work and planning if it is to be done well. Once this work is done, you can relax and enjoy the rest of your life, however long it may be. This is what we hope this book will help you with.

Chapter 3

How do I tell them?
Breaking the news to children and adults

Gaby Eirew

Telling family and friends that you may not be around for much longer is hard – and dealing with their reactions can be harder.

Many of us feel we can just about contemplate, perhaps even accept, dying and our own mortality, but the thing that fills us with most sadness is telling our children, partner or parents, and knowing how our death will affect them and their lives.

If you have a particular friend or advisor with whom you normally talk things through, consider contacting them and working out how you want to tell people.

In this chapter, I provide you with some good strategies for telling all the people close to you. Be aware that there is a wide range of 'normal' reactions to bad news, and for a variety of reasons, some people may offer difficult, unexpected, and even sometimes downright odd responses. Many responses will be shocked but loving. Some are articulate, others less so, and when I describe the range of children's normal reactions to such news, you may find your families are not so clear in expressing themselves either!

> *Telling friends and family you may not be around for much longer is hard – and dealing with their reactions can be even harder*

We often worry that once we start telling people we are not going to live for long, they will radically change how they behave towards us. We fear we will feel patronized, and lose the normal relationships we have with friends, family and colleagues. However, I find that – save for the first few days after hearing the news – most people tend to stay in their role in relationship to others.

It may be up to you to lead the way and start the conversation. Explain that whilst you are dying you want the same humour, openness and whatever it is that you cherish so much from that friend or relationship. How you act will determine the tone of subsequent conversations.

I remember driving round to a friend who knew time was getting very limited. He was in his early 20s and had an aggressive leukaemia with no bone marrow donor matches found. But as soon as I arrived, all patronizing thoughts flew out of the window as he gleefully came into the hospital car park, sat on my car and started talking books, jazz and politics – just as we normally did. Eventually, tired, he had to go back in, but David was still completely David, even when he was so sick. And you are still you.

What do you say to people?

We have come a long way since the 1950s and 1960s when many doctors felt that it was 'inhumane and damaging to the patient to disclose bad news'. Now people are told about their condition's expected course. I believe this is right, as it gives people the opportunity to use the time they have, in order to have the end of life they want.

I have seen people who have wanted to talk about and share their approaching death very candidly and immediately. Equally, I've seen situations where one or more family members don't want the death discussed or disclosed at all. There have even been times when an adult has died without being told he was dying, as the family chose things to evolve that way and the staff in their hospital agreed. Thankfully, this is increasingly rare.

> ### *Telling people is difficult, but not telling is worse*

Keeping up a pretence that everything is fine is exhausting mentally and physically. When I told very experienced hospice staff, Inbar Shai and Scott Jones, about this book, their first request was that we should encourage people to talk about their condition and to not waste precious time pretending things are fine. Having seen a lot of end-of-life dynamics, I sit firmly on the side of openness and giving everyone the chance to say goodbye, to have the death and conversations that you want.

'But I worry about upsetting people...'

Some people avoid talking for fear of upset. Maybe there has seemed to be no place for talking, in the relentless quest to get better. That is understandable, but I feel that beyond a point, you may be doing yourself and your family a disservice by not being open. It may rob you of the special conversations; that transition to focus on living well now and eventual closure that everyone can benefit from. Worse, it can make children and those close to you look back with sadness at lost opportunities to connect more and discover deeper.

Friends and family who are not advised of a person's impending death may develop a distrust of those close to them. At very least, they will probably regret that you did not lean on them by talking openly and honestly. They might be hurt because they feel excluded. You may wish to withhold information from people in an attempt to protect them, but they may take that differently and feel they have somehow failed, by not giving enough to you or not being close enough.

Talking about death before someone dies gives us the chance to think it through and allow everyone to process what is happening. It also gives us the opportunity to talk about what needs to be done and said, as well as the practical issues of getting people in other parts of the country or the world in contact, in case their presence or input is wanted. I was very grateful to have been able to get back from Canada to England when my father was dying, something that would not have been possible had he not been open from the start.

Dying can often fast-forward people towards what and who really matters to them. Acknowledging that time is very limited, can make both sides more amenable to settling old scores or enabling contact with people who are key.

When will you tell them and what will you say?

When to tell people you are dying is up to you. You may need support from the start and want to tell everyone as you see them, or you may wish to wait till you have a second opinion and plan how and to whom you are going to speak. Some people want others to pass on the information on their behalf.

I would suggest that just two things should be in place before you tell children:

- you know the diagnosis and prognosis as accurately as possible

- you believe it.

Reach a position where you are able to relax and not withhold truths or have to watch your words. You will be saying to people: this is the situation, I agree it is very difficult, but we can make things a bit more manageable by handling it well.

With most people I know, their fear in advance of speaking is much greater than the reality. Many more people wished they had spoken earlier rather than later, or not having spoken at all.

Telling children

Historically, children were not told about deaths, nor involved in funerals, and many adults were not even told about their own imminent deaths. This is all changing and children's losses and relationships are being recognized. Even so, some people try to withhold the inevitability of their early death from their kids for as long as possible, trying to protect the innocence of childhood. But they are not necessarily helping their children in this way and not telling can lead to understandable and significant difficulties around trust.

As Pippa explained in Chapter 1, doctors can now fairly regularly (if not often accurately) predict our deaths, but we still have to catch up with this emotionally. One of the things that medical advances have brought us is the chance for everyone to say good bye; the chance for people to learn a lesson in trust and work out how they, as a family, get through this together.

> **Many more people wished they had spoken earlier, than later or not at all**

Once you tell your children, they can prepare in some way. It is far worse for them to find out from someone else or from a letter left out at home, or by them Googling your condition. Children are amazingly attuned to changes at home. They also know how to look up information. I asked a doctor if the young family of a patient knew about his condition. 'They know what cancer is,' was the reply. 'They just needed to hear the word 'pancreatic' and look it up.'

Discovering that death is part of life

With young children, it is really helpful if they already have a sense of life cycles before they have to deal with a family member's death. The death of plants in winter, the neighbour's cat dying, are all things that can be acknowledged and spoken about so children understand the cycle and inevitability of death.

As adults, we can communicate that we are born, we try to live well and we will die. *Mayfly Day* by Jeanne Willis, with illustrations by Tony Ross (Penguin 2006), is a wonderful book that teaches children no matter how long our life is, it can be beautiful, through the story of a mayfly, who only lives for one good day. Children who encounter the death of someone close to them, without any understanding of life cycles, will have a much harder time processing what has happened. They will be more likely to keep looking for a 'why?' and catching up on the huge concept of death itself, which can get in the way of their processing and coping with their personal loss.

Most children are also exposed to a huge number of images and negative ideas about death from cartoons and video games. Characters often suffer ridiculously violent deaths, and also often cheat death in equally ridiculous ways. The more that we can be open with children, the more we can reassure them that death happens to all of us eventually, and that your own death will most likely not be either painful or nasty.

Getting support from school

To help you decide what you want to say, you might visit or contact your child's school and speak with the head counsellor or class teacher confidentially. You may want to ask them about how they deal with death and what their suggestions are. You may ask them if they have some good age-appropriate books that your family could borrow. This would be a good time to explain your beliefs, if appropriate, so the school does not say anything that contradicts your and the child's beliefs. Most schools will react with much support and many resources. It is important to let the teachers know of the circumstances in advance, so any changes in your child's mood or behaviour are understood and accommodated, and any absences are followed up quickly.

Once you have spoken with your child, you can then ask the teachers to share the news or not to share it, whichever the child prefers. The child may decide they categorically do not wish to share the information at school, but then share it themselves anyway very soon after, and that is fine and normal. Even if they told you not to share your information with others, know that they will tell and they have to be able to tell. Be prepared – tell them when you are ready for everyone to be told. Most importantly, children going through loss want to be specially and sensitively treated but not singled out at school, and that hard-to-achieve balance is key.

Ways to handle telling children

- You might like to keep the whole family home when you talk to your children. Ideally, find a long weekend and just keep some time for being close and undisturbed.

- It can help to have a good adult friend there for the child to let off steam with and to field any questions they may be worried to ask you – such as 'will it hurt?' 'was it my fault?' It could be a cousin or aunt whom the child can play and talk with. Ask them to let the child lead the conversation and ask them to stay with what is honest, not giving false reassurances.

- Decide whether you're going to tell children one by one or all together – this partly depends on age and maturity. If one by one, have someone on hand so the child does not share the information to the others as they leave the room. You might ask adults not to share the information for a few days or until you advise them, so you can take your time telling people directly and so that others don't hear it on the grapevine.

- Children cannot be asked to keep such a secret for more than a few hours and sometimes the grapevine can be very useful. If you want to share a clear message, after you have told people close to you, you might want to send a letter with what you want people to know.

Here is a nice synopsis of an email a mother sent to her child's school a few days after telling her child that she was dying, as she did not want any misinformation to affect her child. She rang the Head and told her confidentially on a Friday so she had time to develop support. The mother told her daughter the same day, when she came back from school: this was sent around on the Monday:

Thanks: *It is lovely to be part of this community. School and friends mean so much to us.*

History: *I have been sick for a long time now.*

Prognosis: *I understand that I am likely to only have some months left to live.*

Wishes: *Thank you for being there for Kate. I know she really values friendships and especially loves time playing football, board games and going to the park with friends. Your help in picking her up and taking her out with your families has been and will be invaluable. Please understand if we need to change plans as we navigate this.*

Future: *Kate will carry on at school and living at home with Declan as normal. Thank you for passing this on gently to your children.*

Contact: *I will be checking emails sporadically. Thank you for all the kind words. Please contact Sam for anything day to day as she is helping us out a lot. Her email is …*

A similar email could be sent round to friends and colleagues and to partner's colleagues so everyone knows what is happening and what support and contact is wanted. It also sets the tone of acceptance and what you want going forwards.

Be prepared for children to ask lots of questions about what it means for them. Children develop to be naturally and healthily egocentric for the first decade or so. You will hear questions like: Why did this happen to me? What will we do for holidays? Will we still go to the same school? Do we need to change the car? Will we still get Christmas presents? Can I tell Suzy? Will we get the illness too? Did I make you have it? A small child might often ask: 'Will you still be my mum/dad if you die?'

'It's not fair.' How children may react

After a time, I would expect most children of six or above to start by getting angry, as they appreciate what this loss means. 'Why have you got this? … Why me? … It's not fair.'

Even if you are resigned to your prognosis, they are not. You might have contemplated not getting better and they might not have even imagined that. Let them, at least for a while, be angry. It may even help you and others around you who are trying to make a premature peace and holding all the anger in.

Sometimes children attempt negotiation: 'If I am really good, will you get better?' Simply reassuring your children that this condition was not caused by anyone – especially not them – is very cathartic for all.

Younger kids, who are less articulate, will navigate to wanting more physical connection with you. If you can, let them feel reassured by being able to sit on your bed or touch you. For these younger children, you and others may have to repeat your diagnosis, treatments and chances over and over as they try to process it. For kids, so much is transient: they get into a car at home and magically get out somewhere else; they fall asleep in a café, and wake up in their pajamas at home in bed. They will likely ask and re-ask, just to check the details are the same. It is not that they don't remember or don't care, but that they need to keep asking, to understand. They flit between their play world and the real world, and they may be trying to go between their fascination with death and their fear of your death. Don't be sad if they talk about your death in the same sentence as the squashy worm in the park – they are simply trying to make sense of their world.

Older children may attempt to cope or feign being adult enough to not need you. They need, but may shun, physical closeness. They may even start hanging out more at others' houses, pretending to themselves and others that they do not need you. Let them vent and have their usual level of independence, but watch out for any unusual risky behaviours: truanting, abnormal sexual relations, alcohol or drug misuse. You are their parent and they need you. They may mess up for a while. School grades may swing up or down as they may feel that they need to excel, or to give up study, go to work and provide. Conversely, they may feel everything is pointless or veer between the two schools of thought. Their first reaction is often not their long-term reaction.

You may like to share how you sometimes find it hard to cope too, but that you can do it together as a family, and that you will all muddle through together. Remind them that they will not always feel like this, but that it is OK to feel like this now. Tell them that if they don't know something – children sometimes feel alone in not having the answers, assuming adults do – feel comfortable saying 'I don't know.' If you have an approach that helps you cope with what is happening, do share it, but don't impose the same approach on your children.

S.P.I.K.E.S
– A helpful way to deliver bad news

People will be shocked and take time to adjust to the news of your condition. You might have to remind yourself to ignore their instant reactions and know that they will return to a useful supportive relationship for you as soon as they can.

Oncologist Rob Buckman came up with a useful strategy for delivering bad news to people about a cancer diagnosis. It was designed for doctors giving news to patients, but we find it useful in many settings and you might like to use it too, as you give your family's news to people.

His strategy acknowledges good communication and counselling techniques, reminding us not just to tell information but to incorporate the person's expectations and response. Put briefly, SPIKES is a mnemonic for:

Setting – Arrange for somewhere private with the right people present. Try to have everyone sitting down, in good eye contact with each other and with enough time for each other.

Perception – Ask some open-ended questions to get a sense of how accurately the person understands the condition and what they think is happening.

Invitation – See if the person wants to know more information. It is thought that if they ask for it, it may lessen the anxiety of you giving the bad news. They may shun the idea of being given bad news, as a coping mechanism.

Give *Knowledge* – Warning that you have bad news for them can lessen the surprise and help their processing of the information. You could begin, 'I am sorry that I have more bad news.' Remember that during your treatment you may have become familiar with medical terminology which might be opaque to them, for example instead of saying 'metastasized' you may wish to say 'spread', or instead of 'recurrence' you could say 'come back'. Being honest, and open, but not blunt, may enable the person you are talking to, to fully take in the information and let you as a person and you as a family and friendship group move forward. You now want to shift the focus from recovery to symptom control and plans for making the most of the time you have left.

Respond with *Empathy* – They may react with sadness, shock, grief, rejection or silence and this is all normal and understandable. They may want initially to hide their reaction from you. Just because they behave as though it is all fine, does not mean they genuinely believe or feel that.

Strategize and *Summarize* what you and they need – This may happen later. It can be anything from a cup of tea for you both now to planning an amazing trip together in the future.

Take charge of telling

Let people help you. Feel free to tell people if you want to see them more, or less. Sometimes, people hover when they wish to be of support but don't know what to do – give them a job if you can think of one. Others may stay away, fearing they are encroaching.

Answer machines and emails can be a useful ally. A few close friends or relatives could inform more distant people that you do have not the energy to reach out to. Please only take the calls you wish at a time that suits you and your level of energy. If you do decide on an occasional blog, see if you can get a tech-savvy friend to coordinate it. There have been some beautifully honest blogs which live on after their authors have gone:
    penmachine.com (Derek Miller), or
    vanessalafaye.wordpress.com/living-while-dying
are excellent examples.

Telling people does not need to be feared. It can be the important step which brings you support and starts the delicate process of closure you need.

> *Let people help you… Telling people does not need to be feared. It can be the important step which brings you support*

Ideally, telling people will bring your friends, family and colleagues rallying round and giving thoughtful assistance and space as you need it. One hospice founder said instead of hearing 'Look after yourself', imagine they had said 'What one thing can I do so that you can look after yourself?' Then let them help by doing errands, helping with chores, making quiet plans for the future with your involvement or following through with your plans and needs. Once people know what is wanted, they might do it regularly, be it gardening, cooking a meal or picking up children or groceries. People tend to like to help and there are many helpers out there once you ask.

It is important for you to tell the people close to you, but telling and receiving their reactions can initially be very tiring, so pace yourself, take your time and get lots of sleep and support. Decide on a friend, relative or counsellor you can check in with after you have told people, as it will likely make your condition feel increasingly real to you, and it will be good to debrief or chat to someone.

Do it your way; you might want to tell people very close to you yourself, then have friends or family tell others. Many people tell their closest loved ones and then focus on the time ahead.

The word will get around; whilst this might feel odd, it is also inevitable and fine if the facts are passed on. Some people prepare a letter that they get circulated at work or ask a close colleague to tell everyone.

There is no right or wrong. This is your life, just as it is your death, and how you approach it and the onus you place on things of importance, is totally for you to decide.

Updating people

For adults and children, it can be useful to have a helpline number or website address to produce if people want to know more, so you don't need to keep repeating your condition and details. Some people choose to blog or email out to friends how they are doing; that is fine if you want to, but let it be an occasional thing so you are under no pressure to write regular updates.

Enjoy and share with your children

Reflect on what has been, what will be and how much you love them. Celebrate what abilities and attributes they have.

A project that can be done with children is making dolls with your old clothing, so in future each child can have a familiar doll with your smell and look. They can remember making them with you and the dolls will be there to hug when you are not.

Best of all, ask your children what they want to do with you (ask before you agree). Brainstorm what you want and can do together with the time you have now and refer to that often, so you can use this time to have good experiences and strong memories.

They may like to dance together on a video. They may want to go to Disney or the beach with you, to watch old movies together, to play a board game or to choose the colour of their bedroom walls with you. One 16-year-old boy wanted his mum, dying with bowel cancer, to choose the clothes he should wear at her funeral. They talked, laughed and cried their way through that discussion. He could not plan everything with her, but he could start that first step of considering life once she was dead and he was grateful for that opportunity.

Structures of support

You will get help and support from friends, family, colleagues, medical staff and support groups. Chapter 16 will tell you about some amazing groups available. If you can, reach out to start a web of help and guidance for you and your family which can give support both now and into the future. This will both reassure you and give them a gentler transition. They will learn that any good person who comes into their life is not trying to replace you, but to be there in addition.

Getting and accepting support from terrific groups will show that you can accept help too, which is an important sign of strength. Some groups will invite you to a regular session, other groups will send you volunteers, who get to know you, as well as becoming familiar to your family early. There are some wonderful people who get to know a family, perhaps make a personal poem or piece of art with that family, and give support far into the future; that sense of knowing the whole family and continuity can give much solace.

If you can access one, a support group specifically for children can be very helpful. I was supporting one group of children when a boy of 10 came up to a girl he recognized from school. He quizzed her quite a lot about school and the recent death of her mum. She answered very matter of factly until he stopped, smiled and walked away; he was now convinced that a schoolmate had truly lost a parent just like he had. His bravado gave way to his feeling of some peace that he was not suffering such losses alone and after that first awkward encounter, he spoke gently and they talked supportively to each other.

Establishing routines

Your child may act up a lot but maintaining routines and family values, as much as you are able, is important. Your child may need to find release and that might be in karate or shoe throwing. They need that but they also need to know that their life will go on and that they will be supported, loved and safe.

Telling people about death enables us to plan and try out what the future will look and feel like. There may begin to be more contact with a grandparent or the other parent who will be looking after them. If mum has always picked them up from school, starting the transition with another person collecting them, may get the child used to the new system and the other adult more familiar with the school and staff. If you are still able to do the school run and want to, consider doing it together.

The Ostrich and the Hedonist – how adults may react

When dealing with someone close dying, people (both children and adults) can say the sweetest and warmest as well as the weirdest things. If it is the latter, try to forgive them.

Many adults actually have quite similar needs to children and, when told, can act in similar ways: wanting support for themselves, not believing the prognosis or wanting to know how your death will affect them. I think our lack of experience and general societal shortfall around death means that sometimes even the kindest people, in situations of stress, can mess up and say or do the darnedest things.

One woman with ovarian cancer told me that her friends turned for a while into somewhat cartoon versions of themselves. She called them:

The Grim Reaper – the person who could only talk about her death.

The Witchcraft Gal – the friend who wanted her to save herself by eating special foods and seeing specialists in far flung corners of the world.

The Selfish One – who wanted to talk about how bad the death would be for her (the friend!) – yes, really!

The Ostrich – the friend who wanted to ignore everything about the illness.

The Religious Zealot – who wanted her to get baptized and save herself.

The Hedonist – who just wanted them to party with the time left.

The Amazing – friends who just stayed the journey's ups and downs, tears and laughter.

I wish you The Amazing.

Chapter 4

Time to travel
The practicalities of travelling with illness

Dr Pippa Hawley

If you ask people what is on their bucket list, you will invariably see at least one travel wish: cruising the Inside Passage to Alaska, visiting the Galapagos Islands, Antarctica or other far-flung parts of the world. Closer to home, Disneyland is on many people's list, especially children's of course: a trip to one of the Disney theme parks is the most common request that the Make a Wish Foundation funds. My personal bucket list has always been at least half travel-related, and though I have already ticked off many of the trips, I invariably add another one or two each time I get home.

Becoming seriously ill compresses the time available to complete your bucket list travel dreams, but it can also give people the impetus to get on with them. The downtown Vancouver hospitals regularly admit patients who have been transferred from cruise ships, and I have met a number of cruise passengers who were within the last weeks of life. These people were fully aware that they may not live long enough to get home, but were totally happy with that, having planned for the worst, and hoped for the best'. They were hugely satisfied with their travel experience (despite ending up in hospital) and wouldn't have missed it for the world. I have made the Inside Passage trip myself and can totally understand why they felt they could not die without having had a chance to see the whales, mountains, waterfalls and glaciers. Swimming with the salmon in a wetsuit filled with hot water is an experience I would highly recommend to anyone!

> *Becoming seriously ill can give people the impetus to fulfil their travel dreams*

There are also many people who wish to travel back to their home town to die, sometimes for practical reasons, such as being with family and friends who can care for them, and sometimes just for a sense of completeness. There is a spiritual aspect to being laid to rest where you came from, in the culture and with the rituals that are important to you. It can help you feel that you are completing the natural circle of life.

The practicalities

Travelling can, however, be very difficult when you are not well. Changes in routine and time zones can play havoc with your medication administration schedule, your bowels and your sleep-wake cycle. It can put you in a situation where you do not have access to the medical care team who know you, even sometimes into situations where there is no medical care at all. There may be physical restrictions that make things uncomfortable for you, such as less oxygen in the air if you are in high mountains, or in a plane.

When you start thinking of all the worst-case scenarios the panic can escalate. What if I don't like the food? What happens if I have to go to hospital? What if I lose my medication? What if my flight is delayed? How will I get insurance? What if I get diarrhea and the toilets are awful? What if I die overseas?

The perceived problems can become so overwhelming that many people just give up and never achieve their travel goals. But travel is possible, if that is what you want, and this chapter will give a guide to how to approach a bucket list travel wish, outlining the steps you need to consider when planning your trip, and some practical strategies which may help you overcome the panic of 'what ifs'.

The first step – a plan

Planning for the worst and hoping for the best is a good principle when preparing for any event, especially a trip. Having a plan which includes all the worst-case scenarios does not make them any more likely to happen, just as making a will or buying life insurance does not make you any more likely to die. However, it might feel like a hurdle that has to be overcome. Having to draw up a plan for your travels can be the trigger which forces you to confront all the possibilities in your future, and this can be hard at first. Once done however, many people experience a tremendous sense of relief and an uplifting sense of calm. The 'elephant in the room' has been acknowledged, and the conversations triggered by the need to plan for the trip can have benefits which positively affect many other aspects of life and relationships.

The process of trying to plan for a long dreamed-of trip can also lead to increased awareness of other priorities. You might realize that other things on your bucket list are actually now more important to you. It's perfectly OK to go through the process of planning a trip, then change your mind and switch to something else entirely!

Get informed

It is important to become as well informed as possible about your destination in order to be able to plan properly for all eventualities. If you have always been a relaxed kind of traveler, comfortable that you can cope with the adventures and surprises of the open road, now is the time to be more organized.

Checking out your destination: potential sources of information

- Travel guides such as the Lonely Planet series
  – a great start, but some details will inevitably be out of date.

- Travel websites
  – can be excellent, but beware. If they are run by a company trying to sell you a holiday, they won't mention any hazards or drawbacks.

- Official government websites
  – can be less than helpful, sometimes providing apparently fictional information, and again omitting to mention important dangers to be avoided.

- People who live there or who have recently visited
  – these will provide the best information. Talk to any contacts you can find, and use a travel agent who specializes in that area. Look at on-line reviews as well as official websites, so that you get a good variety of viewpoints. Sites such as TripAdvisor have a lot of traffic and tend to be reasonably accurate. Reviews are dated and they also have the option for you to post questions about specific properties, such as how far is it from the airport? Is it wheelchair friendly? Is there a working fridge in the room? What vaccinations are needed? Try to double check with the property manager if you can.

I was able to give advice to a patient planning a trip to the British Virgin Islands in the Caribbean. They were planning to land at the airport after a long flight from Canada and take the last ferry of the day to their dream hotel destination. However, I had recently made a trip to that same place and discovered that the ferry schedule is more 'wishful thinking' than an actual timetable. The chances of that ferry actually being there when advertised were slim, and certainly not to be counted on. My patient and their family were able to change their plan to include an overnight stopover between islands, being sure of having a stress-free journey with lots of room to enjoy the laid-back Island Time they were so looking forward to. We were also able to help them choose a hotel for the stopover which was on top of the hill overlooking the port, as the heat and lack of breeze down at sea level would be stifling and very difficult to acclimatize to when coming straight off the plane from the frozen north.

These may seem like small things, but they can make the difference between a miserable time and a wonderful trip.

Asking for help

Allowing enough time is key to stress-free journeys when you are ill. Make sure that you allow extra time for every connection, preferably organizing for somewhere to lie down. If there is more than a couple of hours of time difference, try to factor in an overnight stop to help adjust, and to allow for unforeseen delays. Airports usually have a lounge which, for a fee, you can stay in between flights, often with food and drinks included. These may only be accessible if you fly on certain airlines, or have enough frequent flyer points, so it is important to find out about them in advance.

> ***Allowing enough time is key to stress-free journeys when you are ill***

Asking for help can be hard for people who are used to being independent, but letting the airline or airport know in advance that you need help can make a huge difference to your experience. Passengers can have wheelchair assistance even if they can actually walk for short distances, and this allows you to take hand luggage (including duty free) which you might not otherwise be able to carry. It also often gets you whisked to the head of the queue at passport control!

Having an emergency contact can be invaluable. Travelling through Australia many years ago, I used an emergency number thoughtfully provided by one of my mother's colleagues whose parents lived there. I arrived in Sydney with such rip-roaring tonsillitis that I could barely speak, after three months in the Solomon Islands as a medical student. Fortunately, I had the emergency number. My mum's friend had told these lovely people that I might call, and hearing me croaking feebly down the phone, they realized this was an emergency, and swooped down to take care of me. They picked me up from the bus station, tucked me up in bed, got a doctor to visit, fetched my antibiotic prescription, fed me ice cream until I could swallow chicken soup, and then spent the rest of the week showing me the delights of Sydney and the surrounding area. I don't know what I would have done without that little piece of paper with the phone number on.

That brings me to a recurring theme in this book: let people help you. We were able to show my new Australian friends some hospitality in return a few years later when they visited my family. In fact, my family has a long history of paying it forward by taking in 'strays' from all over the world, still keeping in touch with many of them today.

Problems with air travel

Though flying is fast and the safest form of transport, there are some situations where flying is not the best choice, and alternatives have to be considered. Modern airplanes keep the cabin pressure at the equivalent of being between 5000 and 8000 feet above sea level. The pressure change when travelling from ground level (usually at or near sea level) causes two problems: expansion of gas pockets trapped in the body, and reduction in the amount of oxygen available to the body from breathing.

If you have just had surgery there may be pockets of air inside your body that can expand up to 30% in volume, which can be extremely painful. Normally gas escapes gently from the top or bottom ends of your bowel or is breathed out, but it can be very painful if you cannot equalize the pressure on each side of one of your eardrums when taking off and descending. A blocked sinus can be excruciating when the air inside the sinus expands and can't get out. This is one of many reasons why flying with a head cold is a bad idea! Trapped pockets of gas in the chest are particularly dangerous. There are also problems if you have had brain surgery. If in any doubt, check with your doctor first.

Shortage of oxygen can create serious difficulties. If you are barely maintaining an adequate oxygen level in your blood and then have the added the stress of having to work harder to get the oxygen in, you can become unwell during the flight. Your heart and brain can struggle to function properly. If you have heart failure you can work your heart too hard and end up with fluid backing up into your lungs, causing shortness of breath, or into the veins and tissues in your lower body, causing swelling. You could become confused if your brain is not getting enough oxygen. This can be overcome by breathing additional oxygen, but you need to plan for this to make sure the airline has sufficient oxygen supplies for you to be able to breathe it for the whole flight.

Medical Aspects of Travelling
Blood clots

People who have cancer often have a predisposition to getting blood clots in the legs, and it is a good idea to speak with your doctor before any travel that requires you to sit still for an extended period. A preventative injection of an anticoagulant, or even just a tablet of aspirin, may be wisely considered, unless there is a risk of bleeding from an exposed blood vessel.

A blood clot in the leg veins is known as a deep vein thrombosis or DVT and can cause an uncomfortable swelling and redness of the calf. More importantly however, part of the clot can break off and circulate through the heart, lodging in the blood vessels going to the lungs. This is known as a pulmonary embolism (PE) and symptoms can range from a big one causing sudden death, to smaller ones causing chest pain, shortness of breath, and coughing up small amounts of blood.

In addition to taking anticoagulant medicines (also known as blood thinners), the proneness to clotting can be reduced by keeping well hydrated, and keeping your legs moving. Take every opportunity to stretch your legs, wiggle your feet up and down, and walk up and down the aisle. Compression stockings have now improved to look like normal socks and can be bought from most pharmacies and medical supplies shops without a prescription (with a prescription they may be covered by your medical insurance). They are comfortable and effective at preventing the blood from pooling in the calf veins where it might start to clot.

Conversely, when taking the anticoagulant warfarin, for example if you have an artificial valve in your heart, travelling can affect your clotting level and you may require dose adjustment. Ginger can also interact with warfarin and may be taken by accident as an over-the-counter treatment for travel sickness. Do not take any new medicines or foods that might have an effect on your medicines whilst travelling. You need to know what these are before you leave, just in case you encounter them. Imagine you are an Olympic athlete required to do periodic drug tests, and nothing gets past your lips without being checked!

Medications and travel

Travelling when living with illness usually requires that you take along a variety of drugs. These may include opioid-based pain medications, such as morphine or methadone, which may be restricted in the country you are going to.

It is very important that you do not become separated from your medicines during your trip. Some precautions you should take are:

- Take enough with you

- Keep them in their original labelled containers

- Be aware of potential interactions

- Take a letter from your doctor which specifically lists your medications

- Keep them in your hand luggage

- Avoid having to carry liquids.

Ensure you have sufficient supplies of all your medicine, plus enough to allow for unexpected delays or dose increases. This is particularly important for pain medicines used on an 'as needed' basis, as you may find that your pain gets worse while you are away, for example because you are doing a lot more walking than usual, or have been on a bumpy car ride, and you could use up your entire supply before you get home. Though it may be easy to obtain supplies of pills for blood pressure, infections or diabetes in most parts of the world, pain medicines are often strictly controlled and may be simply unavailable.

Keeping pills in their original containers will not only ensure they are kept clean and dry, they will also be readily identifiable and the instructions for use will be clear to anyone who might need to treat you without the benefit of having your medical records. For the same reason, it is helpful to take along a summary of your medical condition and current management plan. The note from your doctor justifying your medicines for customs purposes can do double duty for this. You should also have available a note documenting your goals of care, i.e. what you would want your care providers to do in the event that you became catastrophically unwell for some reason. This might be in the form of an Advance Care Plan or Advance Directive (see Chapter 5). This document should always be with you, and extra copies with your travelling companions. It's not much use in your hotel safe if you have just been hit by a taxi and are in an emergency room where nobody speaks your language! Allow sufficient time for your doctor at home to provide this document well before you leave, as it takes time and information-gathering. Your doctor's surgery may charge for this service but it is well worth the money.

It is surprising how often travellers get separated from their checked luggage, sometimes permanently, so don't take any risks by packing essential supplies in your checked bags. Prescribed medications are exempt from the 100ml liquid restriction currently standard worldwide, but you can get held up in security having to explain what you have, to present documents and so on, so even if you have to pay extra for a tablet form of your normally liquid medicine (for example cough syrup, short-acting morphine, methadone) ask your pharmacy to get you some pills instead. There will be no worries then about refrigeration, leakage, contamination or other issues. There are very few medicines that are not available in a solid (pill or capsule) form. Injectable medicine would not usually be dispensed in large enough volumes to ever be a travel concern, but if you are on intravenous or tube feeding it will be necessary to arrange for supplies to be waiting for you wherever you are heading, again well in

advance. Inhalers are not restricted, but it is important to make sure that, like all medicines, they are clearly labeled and you have documentation to support them.

One memorable patient of mine sailed his boat from Vancouver down the coast of Washington, Oregon and California, heading for the Baha Peninsula, with multiple small packages of his powdered pain medicine sufficient to last him until he could check in with another care team in the US or Mexico. In this form, the medicine would stay fresh without refrigeration and not take up too much space on the boat.

In addition to the challenges of making sure you have access to your medications when travelling, do make sure that there are no predictable effects of travel on your medications, especially flying. At altitude, some medications are metabolized at a slower rate than at ground level, which for most short flights has no real consequence, but on longer flights and for some particularly susceptible medications, the effects can become noticeable. Avoid any alcohol when flying, and if you start to feel unexpectedly sleepy you may need to hold off on taking some pain medications or sedatives for longer than would be your normal schedule.

If you are unlucky enough to pick up a bug and have diarrhea and/or vomiting, the absorption of medications from your bowel may be impacted, and you may need to take extra medication until the problem has passed. Try to find out from your doctor before you leave what to do in the event of this happening, but if in any doubt, seek advice locally. If you are not well to start with, what would normally be a minor inconvenience could be a catastrophic experience. It is very reassuring to have a plan ready for a worst-case scenario, just in case, so you can relax and enjoy your trip.

Dealing with time changes

If you are planning a short trip and have medications which are important to take at set times of day (for example every 8 hours), you may find it easier to just stick to your home time for medications, even if it means setting an alarm to wake up in the night. For longer trips where it would be easier to adjust to the local time, try moving your medication administration times in stages, half an hour or one hour a day, even starting before you leave, so that any change is of minor impact. Adjusting back when you get home can be done the same way.

Travelling with oxygen

Most medical oxygen supply companies have links with their colleagues around the world and can arrange for oxygen to be made available for you in many places. Portable oxygen tanks for use in transit have limited capacity, but there are now models that squirt a little out only when triggered by your breathing in, rather than emitting a continuous stream of oxygen that is mostly wasted. These devices can last a lot longer than the continuous stream ones and may allow you to get from A to B with your own supply. Oxygen concentrators or tanks can be set up in advance to welcome you at your destination, before your portable system runs out. Arrangements of course will vary a lot from place to place, and company to company, so allow plenty of time to plan for this. Many people are fine being off oxygen for short periods, but if you are totally dependent on oxygen this is much more difficult to do, though not impossible. Try going without your oxygen at home for a while before your trip, so that you know how long you can manage without it in the event of an unexpected delay. Knowing that running out of oxygen is not going to lead to immediate symptoms is very reassuring, and the lack of panic will also reduce your oxygen consumption and actually improve your ability to tolerate a break in supply.

Being at altitude reduces the amount of oxygen in the air even in pressurized modern planes, and the flow rate of your oxygen may need to be increased a little whilst in the air, or even if travelling over a mountain range by car or rail. Having a portable oximeter machine can be helpful in deciding whether this is necessary or not. This is a small device you attach to your finger, which displays the percentage saturation of oxygen in your blood. They do need to be calibrated regularly, so if you are planning on getting one, do a trial run with it before your departure, so you know how to work it and what your normal saturation is, and make sure it is checked for accuracy regularly.

Travelling on dialysis

Believe it or not, it is not out of the question for someone needing dialysis to travel. The people who provide hemodialysis have a sort of network of communication and may be able to set up dialysis for you on holiday. This includes some cruise ships, specially set up to run in specific time periods with the necessary staff and equipment provided on board. A good travel agent should be able to figure out what your options are, and the cost may be surprisingly reasonable, even covered by your medical insurance. The patient and family usually handle peritoneal dialysis, with no need for trained staff to be available, and sufficient supplies of the special fluid and equipment can be arranged to be available at your travel destination with sufficient planning.

Other technological challenges

Total parenteral nutrition (TPN, or intravenous feeding) can sometimes be managed long term in people who do not have enough functioning bowel to be able to sustain themselves via eating and drinking. The special feeding solutions are personalized to the individual, and need to be fresh, so there are challenges to travelling far from your home base. If you are on TPN you may still however be able to travel, by having your team of nutrition professionals explore their network of colleagues and arrange for transfer of service on a temporary basis. One of my patients on long-term TPN used to travel regularly to Spain, where the local health services were able to manage her needs very well. Similarly, one of my patients had an implanted pain pump that needed re-filling every month, with special hyper-concentrated sterile pain medicine. She was able to have this looked after for a prolonged visit to Iran, by having her Vancouver team find out who provided that service in Iran. There are many other life-prolonging medical procedures that are highly specialized and sometimes uniquely adapted to an individual, and the prospect of travelling with them may seem completely unthinkable. This may well be the case, but there is no harm in asking, and you may be very surprised at how accommodating people (and your insurers) can be.

In general, people understand that being able to travel for a bucket list trip, especially for family reunification, is vital to many people for good quality of life, and they are usually only too happy to make it happen. Just as allowing your family and friends to help care for you is a gift from you to them, allowing travel and medical professionals the satisfaction of using their special skills to make you happy is a valuable and memorable gift to them.

Insurance

It can be impossible or very expensive to get travel insurance if you have a serious pre-existing condition, and at the end of the day, insurability may determine whether your trip can go ahead or not. There are however some policies which can be set up for you which are reasonable, especially if you have been stable for a while. One thing to watch out for is the length of the stability clause, which is usually 30 days. This applies to stopping medicines as well as starting, so try to make sure that your medicines are fine-tuned at least 30 days before your scheduled departure. Check that it isn't three months, as that is occasionally the rule. Don't try to 'trick' the insurance company by not declaring something, even if it seems irrelevant, because it could invalidate your insurance and you will have wasted a lot of money!

A person might be aware that dying on their trip is a possibility, but this does not have to be a catastrophe if prepared for. Do your family a favour and make sure you have left specific instructions as to what you want done with your body when you die. If you don't care where your final resting place will be, tell them that, so that the expense of repatriating your body can be avoided, but remember that there may be significant costs for disposing of your remains overseas, and it may be cheaper to be sent home if repatriation is covered by your insurance. Using a good insurance broker can save you a lot of money and worry. Ask around your medical condition community and see who has been helpful to others with your needs.

There is an insurance company (MedJet Assist www.medjetassist.com) which covers transport from a hospital anywhere in the world back to the traveler's hospital of choice in their home country, if this is Canada, the USA or Mexico. There are no exclusions for pre-existing conditions for those under 75, and you can buy policies from anything from a week to five years. There may be similar companies based in other parts of the world. Always go through an insurance broker to make sure that the insurance product you buy is going to meet your needs.

Travel agents

Some travel companies specialize in holidays for seniors or disabled people. Expand Your World Travel is a Canadian example, and Accessible Travel a British one, but there are similar companies in many other countries, and some travel agencies may be able to help a lot even if they don't advertise themselves as specialized in this field. These agencies offer support for people wanting to travel with a variety of potential challenges, including diabetes, sleep apnea (needing a breathing machine), being dependent on a wheelchair or scooter, incontinence, needing to take an assistance dog along, being blind or hearing impaired, requiring oxygen, being on dialysis, having an intellectual disability such as autism or dementia, or having a seizure disorder. At the second Bucket List Festival in Victoria, a representative from Expand Your World described (amongst other examples) a trip to Machu Picchu completed by a young man who was not only confined to a special recumbent wheelchair, but had to remain horizontal at all times. Despite the distance to Peru and the altitude (2,430 metres, or 7,970 feet) he made it up and down safely, with some muscular friends gladly doing the heavy lifting.

A good travel agent's experience can be invaluable. The most important thing is to ask: it's amazing what can be done to help you make your dream trip, once people know what you need.

Chapter 5

Putting you in charge
Advance care planning and substitute decision makers

Dr Pippa Hawley

The days of doctors keeping serious medical diagnoses from patients are gone now, for the very good reason that this policy does not help the patients or their families. When people have a sense that what may lie ahead for them is different to their expectations, they generally change their plans accordingly. They live their lives differently. By denying patients the opportunity to do those bucket list activities and have those important conversations, doctors now understand that they would not be doing their patients any favours.

You may already have had your 'bad news', or by reading this book you are in a way anticipating it, so congratulations on being smart and getting prepared. Now we need to talk about what it means to change your plans accordingly.

First it is important to have an understanding of the big picture.

> *What is actually wrong?*
>
> *How does this condition generally progress?*
>
> *What are the chances that it might be cured?*
>
> *What might life be like after treatment?*
>
> *If it isn't curable, how will it affect me?*
>
> *How might I die?*

These are the sorts of questions you should be asking your doctor, and if they don't get answered, you need to keep asking until you feel that they have been addressed. Sometimes expectations can be quite confidently stated, but sometimes it really is hard to tell, and the answers from the experts may genuinely be: 'I really don't know'. This is better than platitudes like 'Don't worry, it will be fine'. As time goes by, the predictability of your future generally gets easier, in terms of knowing what specific challenges you might face, as discussed in the chapter on prognostication. Understanding the big picture is therefore a process rather than an event.

Sometimes a picture says a thousand words, and this diagram may make the process easier to understand. It is called the Bow Tie Model and is a sort of map of how you will progress through your illness, whatever it is.

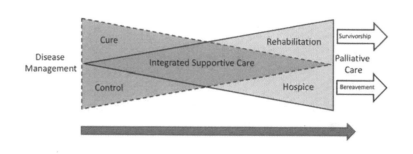

Palliative care is appropriate at all stages, whatever the goal of disease management at the time.

The triangles on the left represent the medical management of your illness, and the triangles on the right represents the care directed to you, the person with the illness. As time goes by, the outcome of treatment of the disease will become clear and you will recognize that your body is either heading for a cure (or at least long-term control) or succumbing to the illness. The focus of care will gradually transition from disease management to either recovery and survivorship, or toward maintaining quality of life in the face of disease progression and then in dying. You can place yourself where you think you are now on the model, and as time goes by you will see how you are progressing through your illness journey.

Eventually we will all end up in the bottom right hand corner, even if it takes a few cycles through the model as we live through various illnesses. But, when your time comes, you can be prepared, and hopefully you will have had time to tick off your big bucket list wishes.

The triangle of medical treatments may become increasingly burdensome and decreasingly effective, and you may decide that you would prefer to forego some treatments.

Advance care planning and living wills

Advance care planning may lead to creation of an actual document, known in most places as an advance care plan or advance directive. Some might call it a living will. The legal status of advance directives varies from country to country, but even if not recognized legally, a clear statement of your wishes will be of great use to your family and to your care providers in the event of a sudden catastrophic health event.

Health care professionals respect wishes included in an advance directive, providing they cover the actual situation in which direction is needed. This is where it can get complicated though, as it is impossible to foresee all possible situations, and it is important to not use any ambiguous terms in your document. Having a health care professional involved in the creation of your document will help reduce the possibility of confusion over what you really meant. Terms such as 'heroic measures' are not always specific enough when decisions have to be made about what constitutes 'heroic'. Does 'artificial feeding' include being spoon fed, or having temporary tube feeding to give you time to see if recovery is likely or not after a stroke? Ambiguous wording can lead to conflict between different family members as well as between family and medical staff, when everyone interprets them differently in the context of their own experience, often at a time when people really should be pulling together.

'Scope of treatment' forms

Many places have fairly straightforward medical orders forms that allow you to choose the goals of your treatment. These are sometimes known as MOST forms – Medical Orders for Scope of Treatment – but a variety of terms are used to describe these forms in different

❄ northern health
the northern way of caring

Medical Orders for
Scope of Treatment (MOST)   Page 1 of 1 | *PATIENT LABEL*

Allergies: ☐ None known   ☐ Unable to obtain
List with reactions: _____

Section 1: Code of Status
Note: CPR is not attempted on a patient who has suffered an unwitnessed cardiac arrest.
☐ **Attempt** Cardio Pulmonary Resuscitation (CPR). Automatically designated as C2. Please initial below.
☐ **Do Not Attempt** Cardio Pulmonary Resuscitation (DNR).

Section 2: MOST Designation based on document conversations. (Initial appropriate level.)

Medical Treatments Excluding Critical Care Intervention and Resuscitation	
M1: _____	Supportive care, symptom management and comfort measures. Allow natural death. Transfer to higher level of care only if patient's comfort needs not met in current location.
M2: _____	Medical treatments available within location of care. Current location: Transfer to a higher level of care only if patient/ts comfort needs not met in current location.
M3: _____	Full medical treatments excluding critical care.
Critical Care Interventions Requested. Note: consultation will be required prior to admission.	
C0: _____	Critical Care Interventions exclusive of CPR, intubation and/or defibrillation: Patient is expect to benefit from and is accepting of any appropriate investigations and interventions that can be offered except CPR, intubation and/or defibrillation. Do Not Attempt Resuscitation.
C1: _____	Critical Care Interventions excluding intubation.
C2: _____	Critical Care Interventions including intubation.

Section 3: Specific Interventions (Optional. Complete consent forms as appropriate)
Blood products: ☐ Yes ☐ No   Dialysis: ☐ Yes ☐ No
Enteral nutrition: ☐ Yes ☐ No   Non-invasive ventilation: ☐ Yes ☐ No
Other directions: _____

Surgical Resuscitation Order
☐ WAIVE DNR for duration of procedure and perioperative period. Attempt CPR as indicated.
☐ Do not attempt resuscitation during procedure.

Section 4: MOST Order Entered as a Result of: (check all that apply)
☐ **Conversations/Consensus**
　☐ Capable adult patient   Name: _____   Date: _____
　☐ Representative   Name: _____   Date: _____
　☐ Temporary Substitute Decision Maker Name: _____   Date: _____

☐ **Physician Assessment and:** ☐ Adult/SDM informed and aware   ☐ Adult not capable/SDM not available
☐ **Supporting Documentation** (Copies place on patient chart and sent with patient on discharge.)
　☐ Previous MOST   ☐ Provincial No CPR
　☐ Advance Directive   ☐ Representation Agreement: ☐ Section 7 ☐ Section 9
　☐ Other: _____

Print Name: _____   **Physician's Signature:** _____
Date (DD/MM/YYYY): _____   **MSP #:** _____   **Contact #:** _____
Renewal Date (DD/MM/YYYY): _____
10-111-5171 (LC - Rev. - 04/14)

places. They offer a limited list of choices and can help clarify the goals of care when it is a hard subject to consider, especially if your medical knowledge is very limited and some of the names for different treatments and concepts seem incomprehensible.

An example of a MOST form is shown. You will find that these forms differ even from one hospital to another in the same town, or between two care facilities only yards apart, so they often need to be re-done when you enter a new facility. The intent and core features of them however all are very similar. That may seem tedious but is a good way of making sure that care is consistent with current goals and wishes, as these can change with time and increasing understanding of your situation, and as illness progresses. Ask to update your form if you feel your goals have changed.

Advance directives

The actual paperwork of advance directives varies quite a bit, not just from country to country, but also within countries, so it is important for you to find out what is required where you live.

In some places, two different documents are required:

1) Designating someone to handle your financial affairs when you no longer can, often referred to as Power of Attorney.

2) Designating someone to make health care decisions on your behalf, often referred to as a Representation Agreement.

A hospital or home care social worker should be able to advise you on the specifics which would apply to you, and there should be information available to you from your local health authority or local government websites.

Many countries also have nationally run organizations which provide excellent resources for anyone thinking of making an advance directive. In Canada, the 'SpeakUp!' campaign from advancecareplanning.ca has very helpful information and printable handouts which can be useful to explain to others. In the UK, cancer support charity Macmillan is a useful starting place for advice, applicable to people with other diseases too: www.macmillan.org.uk

The US-based 'Prepare for your Care' organization has a website which has a planning exercise that you can work through, with great questions and explanations to help you figure out what you might want.

There are some excellent videos on YouTube which describe some of the medical treatments really well (e.g. www.youtube.com/watch?v=skzAGEf9bv8). These can help you with decisions about treatments such as cardiopulmonary resuscitation (CPR) that you have never had an opportunity to witness except in TV dramas – in which the likeness to reality may be very tenuous!

Substitute decision makers

The most important part of advance care planning is actually not the production of a piece of paper, but the conversations that happen on the way. An advance directive can never cover all possible eventualities but talking to the person whom you have chosen to speak for you, in the event of your becoming too sick to speak for yourself, can provide them with all the information needed. This person is your 'substitute decision maker'.

'How could I possibly choose between my children?' (or sisters, or parents etc) you might ask. A team of people who care about you can often be trusted to agree on what you would say, especially if you have done a good job of preparing them. But you cannot always be sure about this, so it is helpful to have a single person designated for this prime responsibility, preferably with everyone's agreement. That way the potential for arguments is kept to an absolute minimum. Choosing two people, especially if they don't get on all that well, is a recipe for disaster.

It is helpful to have a single person designated as substitute decision maker

---

If you can't decide who should do the job, how about letting your family decide? That way there can be no recriminations about favouritism or questionable motives. If between you all, you still can't decide, then there may be a legal order of preference in your location. For example, in British Columbia there is a hierarchy for degree of relatedness that is used to help make decisions about medical care in the absence of an applicable prior advance directive made by the patient, or a designated substitute decision-maker, either by a legal document such as a representation agreement, or by consensus among the family. A quick review of this specific area's rules might be helpful in deciding who you might choose, wherever you live and whatever the legal situation is for you.

Under the British Columbia rules, the health care provider must choose a temporary substitute decision maker

(TSDM) from the following list, in order, meaning that if the top person is not available or suitable, they will look to the next on the list, until they reach someone who qualifies.

- the adult's spouse (check your local definition for this if anything but the traditional opposite gender)

- child

- parent

- sibling;

- grandparent

- grandchild

- anyone related to the adult by birth or adoption

- a close friend ·

- a person immediately related to the adult by marriage.

The person chosen must meet certain criteria. He or she must:

- be at least 19 years of age;

- have been in contact with the adult in the preceding 12 months;

- have no dispute with the adult;

- be capable of making the decision required; and

- be willing to comply with the duties of a temporary substitute decision maker.

Note that parents are considered equal, so if your parents cannot agree, it can create conflict to not have designated one as the prime decider. Similarly, if you have multiple siblings or children, it is a good idea to sort out in advance which one of them is willing to take on that responsibility, or which one you feel can handle it the best. You could even designate one for financial matters and another one for health care decisions, if they have different levels of familiarity or competence with the different issues, or so as to not appear to have a favourite.

Let's talk

Discussing a number of hypothetical situations with people can be really useful in giving them a feel for your overall philosophy, hopes and fears. They will then be more confident that they know what you would say, if they could ask you. Sometimes starting this conversation can be difficult, but don't be put off. Don't wait until you are in a health crisis, as it can then be too stressful and the conversation can become too distressing for either you or them. If this happens you won't achieve your goal of being confident that your wishes will be respected.

Having these discussions can be done at any time, but preferably started when you are well, and periodically revisited to make sure your philosophy hasn't changed. There are some great tools available to help. 'Conversation Cookies' are fortune cookies which have an advance care planning question inside instead of the usual vague suggestion about the future (which is most unlikely to apply to you!). They can be used in a number of ways, but it is probably best to have a time set aside, such as a coffee meeting, pub night, or dinner at someone's house, and open one cookie at a time. Everyone can talk about how they might answer that question, and in the process all participants will gain clarity about their own thoughts.

The following is an excerpt from an Advance Care Planning website

Finding an appropriate icebreaker to start talking about end-of-life care can be tricky — for patients, their loved ones, and their health care team. Life and Death Matters, based in Victoria, BC, has developed a sweeter way to get those conversations started.

Conversation cookies look just like fortune cookies – but instead of predicting the future, they ask you to talk about it. The messages within the cookies address hopes and concerns about end-of-life in a fun and interactive way. Some encourage reflection while others promote dialogue about living and dying well – for example, exploring fears around talking about dying, or what you might say if you could speak at your own funeral.

Kath Murray of 'Life and Death Matters' notes that the cookies can be used in various situations. 'They're a great way to get people talking in a family conference setting, or as part of a public education session,' she says. 'Even passing around a plate of Conversation Cookies at a conference can easily stimulate interesting conversations and self-reflection. Suggestions for how to use the cookies are featured on the Life and Death Matters website.
www.lifeanddeathmatters.ca

This Canadian invention has been well received by hospice and palliative care team leaders across the country and in the US. A hospital in Nebraska, for example, is distributing them to their staff and encouraging them to put answers on a display in their main lobby, as a way to promote advance care planning.

Another great tool is a card set called 'Go Wish' www.gowish.org). This is not really a game, but an activity built on sorting a set of 36 cards, each with a short statement about things people often think of as important in the last weeks or months of life. To play the game by yourself you can sort the cards and rank them according to what's most or least important to you, and then explain to people who might be your substitute decision members why you sorted them the way they did. You can also do the sorting in pairs, families or other groups.

The point of the activity is to stimulate conversation about what is important to each other, and why. Many people remark that when they do the activity several times, the way they sort the cards changes a bit, and that this helps them refine their thinking about their values and how they might apply in different situations.

Don't forget that children living with life-threatening illnesses may have a surprisingly insightful understanding of their situation, and even quite small children can have thoughtful opinions about their wishes for their future. Playing games such as Go Wish or having a Conversation Cookie time, in which all the family participates, can be a low-key way of figuring out if your child has thoughts or feelings that would help you if/when the need arises for you to make a decision on their behalf. Knowing that you have made the right decision can be of tremendous solace in bereavement and can help avoid conflict between family members about whether a decision was in the child's best interests.

Chapter 6

Home, hospital or hospice?
Deciding where to be

Dr Pippa Hawley

Health administrators pay a lot of attention to the place where people die. Dying at home is generally felt to be 'A Good Thing'. This is partly because if you ask healthy people where they would prefer to die, they usually say 'at home of course!'. It is also a lot cheaper for the health care system to not have sick people in hospital, because out of hospital the costs of care (both financial and social) are pretty much all passed on to the family.

Neither of these reasons are very sound when you look into them closely. Healthy people are usually thinking about where they would prefer to live, not to die. When you're not actually very healthy, in fact feeling ill, the whole decision-making process looks quite different. There are pros and cons to being at home right to the end, and it is important to understand the options available to you for your last weeks or days of life.

To a great extent this chapter is designed for people living in countries with a fairly sophisticated heath care system. Though many developing countries have some areas with excellent services for end-of-life care, they tend not to be consistently available, and their capabilities may be very much hampered by lack of local people, expertise or available drugs for symptom management. Patients in some countries do not even have access to essential pain medicines such as morphine. Even in developed countries where access to medicines is generally good, there may be parts of the country which are lacking in services. In major urban centres, cancer patients will often have access to outpatient pain and symptom management and palliative care clinics; state-of-the-art pain-relieving procedures; palliative care specialists who will do home visits; and a choice of residential hospices. There are also palliative care units in most community hospitals. In contrast, a person living in a rural area may not even have a family doctor, and their nearest hospital may be many hours away over difficult terrain, potentially inaccessible for months of the year.

For those with diseases other than cancer the services available may be much more restricted. These terms describing different services may be interpreted differently in different places, or even by different people in the same place, as the use of language in this area has changed over the last few years. For example, 'hospice' used to be another word for 'palliative care', but now there are important differences between the two. Palliative care is about the prevention and relief of suffering and is a medical treatment separate from treatment of the disease.

This chapter will describe what the various options might look like, so that you can do some research into what is available where you live. The aim is to make it easier for you to weigh up the benefits and disadvantages of each option, or at least understand what you can expect.

Hospice

Hospices are designed for people who are, as close to certain as possible, not going to get better. Hospice care, which may be provided in your own home or another home-like arrangement, focuses on ensuring you are as comfortable and pain-free as possible. Hospice care describes the kind of palliative care appropriate for when treatment aimed at curing or controlling the disease has mostly been discontinued. These treatments might include things like chemotherapy for cancer, or transfusions for chronic anemia. Mild treatments may sometimes be continued if they do not seem to be causing any particular side-effects, or if their discontinuation could lead to symptoms; for example, diuretics ('water pills') to prevent fluid retention in people who have heart failure, or inhalers for people with severe lung disease. Though it would be unusual, some people can even continue to receive dialysis in a hospice setting providing it is not too burdensome and the person is aware that they can stop whenever they wish.

Resting in a typical hospice room. The couch folds out to accommodate overnight visitors.

Though there have been notable exceptions, usually much to everyone's surprise, people accepting hospice care generally understand that there is no longer a possibility of the disease being cured, and their life expectancy is becoming short. Hospice goals of care are to make the patients as comfortable as possible, and to avoid any medical interventions that do not have the potential to make them feel better.

> *Hospice goals of care are to make the patients as comfortable as possible, and to avoid any medical interventions that do not have the potential to make them feel better*

Though it is not uncommon for people to be discharged from hospice, either to go back home again or to a long-term care home if their health stabilizes, the majority of people who move into a residential hospice will die there. In general, hospice length of stay is expected to be less than three months, though there have been many exceptions. Once people are kept warm, fed, comfortable medically, clean and loved, it's amazing how often their health improves. I have one patient who was discharged from hospice and is still going strong more than three years later!

Hospice care can be accessed in a variety of locations, essentially grouped into patients' homes or residential facilities. 'Free-standing' hospices are buildings that have been designed to provide as home-like an environment as possible and may be purpose-built or use re-purposed older buildings. What is most important for any hospice, however, is not the building itself – though many residential hospices are beautiful – but the quality and enthusiasm of the people that work and volunteer there.

Appropriate training and qualification of staff are important, as there is a particular knowledge base and skill-set needed to deal with the issues which might arise when a person is living with an advanced illness. The hospice also needs good management, so that the staff members feel supported and appreciated, looking forward to coming to work, and committed to doing their best. A team of well-trained volunteers can make a huge difference to the hospice experience. Knowing that accepting help with daily tasks of living is not causing a burden to care-givers makes it much easier to accept that help. Many hospice volunteers have had their own loved-ones benefit from hospice care and wish to give back. It helps them to know they are useful.

System-level factors such as adequate funding, access to a sufficiently-sized group of appropriately trained hospice physicians, nurses and other health care professionals are critical for a hospice to run properly. I strongly advise any of you reading this who are not ill yourselves and feel able to do so, to train as a hospice volunteer. Anyone who has visited a hospice will tell you what a difference the volunteers make.

Hospital

Hospitals are designed to cure people with sudden illnesses or injuries. They treat infections with antibiotics; they carry out operations such as hip replacements, heart artery bypasses and removing stone-filled gall bladders. The whole set-up is geared to getting patients better, as fast as possible, and getting them home. As we live longer, hospitals everywhere are under increasing pressure. Patient numbers are growing, while a smaller taxpayer base is available for the services needed to meet the needs of increasing numbers of elderly people. As a result, the pressure to discharge patients after treatment is getting greater and greater, with lengths of stay getting shorter and shorter. People are now discharged much sooner after major procedures than ever before to make way for more patients. Unfortunately, some people are found to have rapidly progressive or advanced conditions that can't be fixed, and are not able to go home again.

Many people die from relatively predictable illnesses in hospital, sometimes very peacefully, but sometimes still receiving invasive therapies which have little or no chance of working. Though recognition of when the 'goals of care' are changing can be timely, unfortunately, too many acute care teams don't know when to stop. Awareness of when to switch the approach to comfort and quality of life rather than attempts to cure is very variable, and some doctors and nurses really miss the boat on this. I have heard stories of families wishing for distressing treatments for their sick relatives to be stopped, and hospital staff being very reluctant to focus on symptoms, seeing palliative care as 'giving up', not knowing that palliative care alongside regular treatments can have a huge benefit.

Palliative care in hospitals

Good palliative care can be provided by the main care team, properly trained and supported, or a specialist palliative care team providing consultation support, sharing the care. Sometimes the patient is assessed by the palliative care specialists and then transferred to a different ward within the hospital to be able to receive more intensive palliative care treatments.

Many hospitals have specialized Palliative Care Units (PCUs) to take care of those patients who are having difficulty with management of symptoms such as pain, shortness of breath, or confusion. The units have specially trained staff who can deal with these kinds of problems. These are often in the nicer parts of the hospitals, such as the top floors ('penthouse

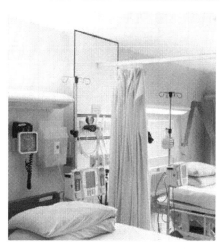

A typical hospital room

suites') or ground level areas next to gardens. Though often decorated more carefully than regular wards, and usually with single rather than shared rooms, these are still hospital units providing comprehensive medical care, including injections and infusions (drips). They often do X-rays, CT scans and blood tests to help figure out what is causing a symptom in order to be able to fix it, or at least to be able to explain what is happening and plan accordingly. Sometimes people die on PCUs if the illness has only just been diagnosed or progresses really fast, but most are discharged once their urgent problem has been dealt with, either back home again, or to a hospice if home is not an option.

Some hospitals don't have a PCU but can create a virtual one in a regular ward when needed. In fact, some small community hospitals provide wonderful palliative care without having a special place set aside in which to deliver it. For some people, especially those with hard to control symptoms such as severe pain, shortness of breath or confusion, or who do not have a comfortable home with a healthy and capable caregiver, a hospital may be the best place to live (and die).

It's the care that is important, not the location.

For some people, a hospital may be the best place to live (and die). It's the care that is important, not the location

---

Home

Those lucky enough to be able to get all the care they need at home can live very well in their familiar environment. Home in this context includes long term care homes as well as your own house. For many people, being able to be in their own home, surrounded by the things they love, can be very reassuring. This is particularly important for people who get confused or who might forget where they are, when to be moved to an unfamiliar hospital or hospice can be very distressing and lead to worsening confusion, restlessness or agitation. If someone wants to stay home, there are a lot of supports available that can make it possible, living well right to the end.

The amount and quality of help available to people needing palliative care at home varies a lot from place to place, and the names of programs also vary hugely. 'Home hospice' is a common term, but some places use locally well-understood labels that work perfectly well. Examples are the Silver Chain program in Australia, or the Macmillan and Marie Curie nurse programs in the UK. The name is irrelevant: as always, it's the quality of care that counts.

It can be hard work to care for someone, especially through a long illness, and caregivers need to look after themselves so that they can continue to be there for their loved one. They need to pace themselves, share the care with others, and know when they need to ask for more help, or even to say that they cannot do it anymore. Promises made in times of relative wellness may not realistically be able to be followed through when situations change.

Company like this is hard to get in a hospital!

When it goes well, living at home right to the end of life can be a profoundly satisfying and moving experience for the ill person and their family and friends. In the next chapter Gaby will suggest many ways to maximize the chance of this going well. Should it go badly, however, it can be deeply traumatizing. Illness is unpredictable and sometimes things can change very fast, so don't feel bad if it doesn't work out for you. A trip to the hospital can be a wonderful relief and is not a failure. If it does work out for you, as it often does, count your blessings!

Chapter 7

Setting up home
Organizing your home to meet your needs

Gaby Eirew

You are unique and have your own ways, passions and preferences. When approaching the end, just as in the rest of our lives, we need our uniqueness and our dignity acknowledged. Some people will want to be alone a lot of the time, some will want close family and friends around them and others will not want to be left alone at all. Most of us will flit between these, often wanting to be with fewer people as time passes and to be with the closest people to us as we get near the last bit.

Having thought about where and how you want to spend the end of your life, if your first preference would be to die at home and it is medically and practically realistic, this chapter aims to help by looking at how best to organize your home. The aim is to have a set-up which can work as your needs change, and can make you comfortable, surrounded by the people and things that matter to you.

You will learn a lot about what you will need – remember also to say what you'd like, even if it turns out not to be possible. If they know what you want, everyone will wish to work towards your goal. Ask and keep asking questions; there is no such thing as a silly question. You will meet a range of professionals who will be happy to tell you what they know to support you. If they don't know the answer, they probably know someone who does.

The impact on your home – prepare for change

Deciding to stay at home will usually involve some significant social and physical changes to your home environment.

The first thing to know is that there will be more people coming through your front door. Nurses will most likely need to come to your home, so one of the first questions is – can you and your family be comfortable with that? Many palliative care educators describe it as a big change for a private person. You may not always have a choice of nurse gender.

While you will have the stability of being at home, your home will be much busier, with more people coming and going. Furthermore, there will probably be many different people. The local health authority will try to offer consistent staff support but, in reality, having the same nursing staff all the time will most likely not be an option. No-one works seven days a week. They should all be able to offer the same high level of help and care as each other, but because of shifts, you might have to get to know a few different people.

At the moment, you may be very mobile, but as you find it more difficult to get out of bed, you might like to give all your main carers a key, if they do not already have one. Different health authorities have different rules on keyholders/dropboxes, so if you don't always have family there to open the door, find out what your health authority's policy is.

Is your home environment suitable?

If you live alone and no-one can stay with you, or if you live somewhere with many stairs or little space, it could be too much of a logistical challenge for you to be cared for at home. If you really wish to be in a home environment rather than in a hospice or hospital, consider staying with family or a friend rather than in your own place.

If your home is small, but you wish to stay there, consider putting some of your things in short term storage or a garage, or putting some stuff you don't need right now in a spare room. This will free up space which might be better used to accommodate large equipment, like an electric bed or a lift. While you need extra things in your bedroom, you may be happy to store away a side table, blanket box and your normal bedside table, to make room for a new bed or a larger table.

The best place for a bedroom

Choosing where your bed will be is really important, as you will spend increasing amounts of time in it. Would you like it moved to the main floor, nearer to a bathroom and toilet? Or is staying in your bedroom important to you? Will you be comfortable having people come visit you in your bedroom? Sometimes an adjustable recliner may even be more comfortable than a bed, and easier to receive visitors in.

Think of the space you have available and how you will spend increasing amounts of time in this room, so choose your favorite place. Many people decide that the living room is the most convenient place to be based, as then people have more space to visit, and other rooms such as the kitchen are more accessible. A living room will probably have a bigger window and space for a television, a visitor chair or a desk. It's a good idea to roll away loose carpets and rugs to prevent trips and slips and to allow for the rolling apparatus that you might need later.

A perfect parlour

Think of the room where you have your bed more as a 'salon' or 'parlour' than your traditional bedroom. The bed will become your primary base for everything and around it you can arrange everything to make it the perfect comfortable and nurturing space:

- Pictures and mementos that mean the most to you

- A table and chair for visitors

- A photo album

- A favourite blanket

- Music, books, magazines, your laptop or tablet, and DVDs

- Your phone and charger, lamp and radio and remote controls and fresh batteries within easy reach

- Plenty of the right pillows and cushions to support your body throughout the day.

Once you have decided on your room, reflect on which way you'd like to face for the best view, watching TV or seeing visitors. If you have chosen to be in a living room, and don't have curtains there, you might want to see if someone could put up blinds or a folding screen over the window, with an easy to use pulley so you can look out when it's light, but have darkness whenever you need to sleep.

Getting the equipment you need

Your doctor and your occupational therapist can advise you on what you might need and send an equipment loan referral for you. Large pieces of equipment like beds, slings and commodes may be delivered by your local service, for example in Canada we have a Red Cross Loan Scheme. Other items may need to be collected from a local depot. You will be given information about how to use the equipment and it will be sterilized when you receive it. For some pieces, like a lift, you and ideally your carers will need to be there when it arrives so you can all be shown how to work the equipment effectively and safely. The equipment should be clearly marked; some people like to put a coloured masking tape on the items, so it is easy to know what came from whom. Most Red Cross equipment is given for free without a deposit – but you might like to offer a donation. If a fee is charged where you live, think about how much easier life will be with the particular piece of equipment, and don't scrimp on anything which will be of use.

When your occupational therapist suggests equipment loans to you, such as a commode, you may feel it is embarrassing or unnecessary. My advice would be – if medical staff think you might need it, take it. You can always put it in a cupboard or throw a blanket over it, but it's better to have it and not use it than not to have it when you need it. Commodes can be fabulous when you feel really weak and the bathroom feels far away.

Most health authorities make no charge for home hospice services. Nursing care and supplies, personal care, and equipment in the home are usually free of charge to eligible patients, but coverage details do vary from place to place. There may be a daily fee for some kinds of hospice care, but the health authority will usually work with you to cover the costs if you cannot. Ask your local home health care service for more information on this. If you have health insurance, it is important that you check with your health plan early, to see what they cover. If you are well off you might even choose to employ someone directly yourself to help provide care or just help with housework and cooking.

Being cared for at home can be quite expensive in additional costs, so do take offers from your care plan, accept friends' prepared meals and borrow safe equipment whenever you can. People like to help.

The other people in your home

Your care will have an impact on the lives of those you share your home with – partner, family, even pets.

Their safety is an issue too: all medications can be dangerous when taken by anyone other than the person prescribed for, so you will need to dedicate an area as your medicine cabinet, out of reach of pets, vulnerable people and children. This can include a lockable/out of reach container in your fridge, if you have medicines that require keeping cool. Ensure too that children can't play with any equipment which has been installed.

You will probably be sleeping more frequently or at different times to others in the household. You might consider changing light bulbs to be softer or to get an additional movable lamp which you can use in bed. If you find your room too dark at night, a plug-in glowing nightlight can be useful.

Sounds around the house are really important too. You want to hear and be heard, but still be able to sleep when you need to. If there is a children's TV or playroom nearby you may find the noise comforting, or it might be intrusive. If necessary, see if the family can temporarily move the play/TV area to give you quiet.

However, you probably don't want to feel isolated in your bedroom. Door wedges are a good buy to hold open the doors (except fire doors), and allow you to remain engaged with others throughout your home when you are resting. Baby monitors offer a robust, inexpensive one-way/two-way speaker system. Alternatively, you could use a handheld chime bell or text messages from your phone, depending on your dexterity, so you can call attention gently when you'd like something.

If you are sitting up and active, and want to be connected to the outside world, see if you can get a phone, radio, TV controls or computer near your bed. Builder's masking tape can be very useful in tying together cables and putting them neatly to the side or along the skirting board without causing any damage to your home and reducing the chance of tripping. If you are feeling tired but like watching or hearing certain programs, write a list of your favourite programs, so if you sleep through some, your carers will know what to switch off, record or leave on.

Ways to help people to help you

A dedicated space for your helping people is important, be they friends, family or nurses. Other things which can be useful are:

- A notebook, clearly labelled on the front, for your healthcare staff to use to communicate with each other and to leave you instructions.

- A visitor book that looks very different, for friends to jot down messages for you. Have these kept in the same place so people always know where to find them and if you miss a visitor, you can still get a message and catch up later.

- A comfortable chair, or even a bed, for visitors so they can be with you day or night.

- Lighting arranged so you can switch on/off a light from your bed easily, while someone coming in to support you can turn on or off a light but not wake you if, for example, they want to care for you or read a book nearby.

- A magnetic board or notice board near the bed is good, to pass on information or to remind you of things, or for you to put anything you need known/posted/collected. You can use half of it for things you cherish too, such as photos and cards, so there is always something nice to look at.

One of the benefits and challenges of being at home is that businesses, friends and family know where to find you and will keep visiting; some may not be aware of your condition.

With a bit of forethought, the outside or the entrance of your home can offer an information and collecting point. Often, friends and family will want to bring round food. If you are not up for seeing people, consider putting a box or cooler box with an icepack at your entrance with a note taped to the top to thank them and to note when someone is likely to be able to bring in the food so it stays fresh. For example: 'Thank you – please leave your generous offering here, we'll collect it at 3pm today'. Subsequent visitors and carers can then bring in offerings as they arrive, put it in the fridge and re-freeze the icepack.

It's important to tell people what you feel like, in terms of visits or supplies.

Coping with visits

Time is very precious but you will need to rest regularly. Although you will enjoy having visitors when you are ready for them, don't hesitate to set boundaries and let people know when you are and are not able to have visits. It's important to be able to say something like:
'It's lovely to see you. I think I may need to rest now.'
'I need to rest for a little, may we catch up next Wednesday?'

You could get an 'Open/Closed' sign from a hardware store to show when you feel like visitors. One lady had a sign to tell people whether she wanted to be visited and what her mood was. 'I wanted to embrace the fact that my mood was all over the place – so people knew and knew it wasn't the normal me. My kids made faces for the poster and I used a 'Learn to tell the time' clock display with moving arms.'

You can make something similar with a card circle with different feelings around the circumference – like 'Happy, Sad, Nostalgic, Sore, Nauseous, Resting, Want to Chat, Want to be Alone' or whatever moods take you – with a big paper clip to point to how you are feeling at that time. When a visitor leaves, ask them to change the clock-face to whatever mood you are now in, so the next people know how you feel.

If you use this clock face idea, do be perfectly frank and have quiet time as and when you need it, so you don't feel you're in the middle of a revolving door!

You will also be connecting with friends and family by phone, as well as in person, and the advantage of this is that it is more under your control. Put an answer message on your phone saying thank you, you are going gently with things at the moment but you will get back to them. You can then call them back when you wake, feeling stronger or simply when you feel like it.

You may wish to have your address book available and phone passcode off or stuck on the front of your phone, so friends can call people with your phone, as and when you request it. Ask any friends who take or make calls for you to note down what people say in the messages/visitor book, so you can look at these later.

Some ways children might be involved when someone at home is very sick

It is important that everyone in the home and family who wants to be involved in caring can be involved, to support the whole unit and feel valued and connected. Feeling part of the help is key and can prevent children from worrying or imagining worse things are going on or feeling sad that they were not included. In case you're not sure about how to involve a child or grandchild, here are some ideas for things they can do, from the youngest child to the oldest:

Younger children

- Sing a song/write a poem/draw a picture for you. Have an easel nearby with a roll of paper where the child can draw

- Make posters to put in the room to cheer you up or pin up photos

- Make decorations. Ceilings are particularly large useful spaces for when people are lying in bed and painters' masking tape should leave no marks.

- Offer hand massage or gentle stroking

- Be the person responsible for bringing a box of tissues, fresh water or ice pops when needed

- Change the TV, radio or music to suit you

- Choose some music – your current favourite, or something from your culture or your youth

- Make something you can enjoy, such as a smoothie or a bowl of ice cream.

Older children and teenagers

- Read from a favourite book or poem

- Write on your whiteboard/in your visitor book about visitors and events that week

- Find some feel-good news stories and put them on a pinboard

- Be responsible for recharging electric gadgets

- Pin family memorabilia like awarded ribbons or postcards on to curtains

- Be a scribe for the person in bed and send any letters/postcards/emails wanted

- Mount cards, letters and nice things people have sent on a board

- Help with the garden or water or bring flowers/ pot plants into your room

- Help organize the Celebration of Life or smaller family celebration

- Come over when texted 'just to hold the fort'.

Much older children

- Escort friends (like seniors, who might have difficulty visiting you) by car, bus or train to visit you

- Make and fridge/freeze simple meals for you.

Food and drink

A huge industry has arisen to try to get people living with life-limiting conditions to eat differently (or buy certain products). There are dubious proven benefits to most of these diets and products, so eat what you enjoy and what makes you feel comfortable. Talk with your doctor and nutritionist about what is right for you – we discuss this in more depth in chapter 10.

If you are staying with friends or family, consider having a shelf in the fridge just for your things, so you or your visitor can access them easily for you. This place can also be used for food that people may drop off for you to eat later.

If swallowing becomes difficult, you may want to have more soups, rice puddings or to use a juicer/blender. Later, ask your nurse for swabs for your mouth, if it feels dry. You may want to have a moisturizer and lip salve, a jug with water and some bendable straws on your bedside table for easy drinking while reclining.

These are all ideas to support your important ideal to stay at home. For the vast majority of us, spending the last stage of our life at home is achievable. We may need to be open to the notion that events may change our plans. If you are not comfortable or your home cannot be altered in the right way, or you have high-tech medication needs you may need to relocate to a hospice, palliative care unit or someone else's home to be more comfortable. It is still your decision and the health staff will do their absolute utmost to ensure you can have what you would like. If you do need to move, discuss with your carers what things to take that are most important to you, from pictures to notebooks, pillows and music. If in doubt, take it.

Chapter 8

Caring for your carer
How to ensure that carers are sustained and appreciated

Gaby Eirew

It is wonderful if you have one or more people caring for you. Caring for a loved one is a very special role: as those people learn to take on more responsibilities with you, and for you, you will need to place your trust in them as you feel less able to carry out your normal activities. Accepting some level of vulnerability and accepting help and support is important. Again, let others help you, but this chapter is where we encourage (in fact, implore!) you to help your carers; you can empower them to look after themselves properly from the outset.

Carers may feel that they want to focus on you to the exclusion of their own needs. But it is not good for either of you if they drive themselves too hard. You can help them by ensuring that they have balance in their days, so they can sustain themselves.

It can be tempting for carers to feel they should negate their needs, but that is neither healthy nor sustainable. You'll want your carer to treat themselves with love and kindness while they navigate supporting you now and having a different future ahead.

They may be tempted to spare you nothing, but whilst this is a lovely sentiment, they can't do everything, or they will get quickly exhausted. Every nurse, doctor or marathon runner takes proper rest from their work. Caring at the end of life is done for love, not money, but rest is still the key to sustainability. In her book *Final Journeys*, Maggie Callanan makes a lovely statement: that she will only allow 'one ambulance per family'. No-one should get sick looking after you! This chapter will help you to help them stay healthy, fit and feeling balanced.

You might feel that your relationship is somewhat one-sided right now, but people become carers because they love you and want to repay your warmth and kindness. You can offer a lot in return by being yourself and encouraging your carer to learn to pace themselves, following a few key tips:

Tips for careful carers

- Have small periods of time away from the caring tasks

- Get exercise and eat properly

- Unless things are critical, the carer should keep important appointments

- Have other people to talk to and relax with

- Access carer groups and support helplines, counsellors and use them

- Have a care package for the carer too which goes everywhere

- Get enough rest.

The teamwork between you and your carer should make it a supportive and satisfying experience for you both. Your gift to them will be in giving them your close relationship as well as a healthy template for how they can look after themselves in the future, including in bereavement.

Just as you may have a book of important appointments, can you encourage your carer to book their important appointments – both proactive and preventative ones? See if you can both get support for the various areas of your life that are key to you, be they physical, social, vocational, emotional or spiritual. You might see if there is a support group which you could join, for example a hospice or cancer care club or a stroke association. Many organizations offer support for the person and their families and carers, so see what's available.

Get connected

Accepting care from someone else from time to time will allow your main carer to have a break, which you might both benefit from. If your carer is concerned at leaving you alone, perhaps you can arrange for a friend or neighbour to stay with you from time to time, instead. People will be happy to, once they realize that your carer needs time to themselves too and that they are fully capable of doing whatever is needed. If your carer is worried, remind them that you can always reach each other by phone. Having outside support established for your carer, while you are ill, is a kind way to ensure that they will have support later, when they might appreciate talking to someone who already knows them (and you).

Ideally, visits from another helper should be short but regular, giving both you and your carer the opportunity to feel in touch with the outside world during this rather unusual time in your lives. Many people will be happy to be invited round and just sit with you and chat, if they know they'd be

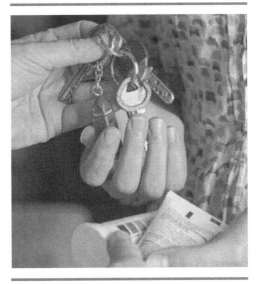

welcome. Very often people are just waiting for an invitation, not knowing what to say or do. Being given a task to do, which they know will be genuinely helpful, will make them feel needed and loved themselves; that is a gift, not a burden.

When you ask them, you can put in a caveat such as, 'If the day is unusual or tiring, I might need to cancel or postpone the get-together.' 'Might you be able to take [your carer] for a coffee instead, if I'm sleeping?' People will fully understand.

You might like to download a video or ask a friend to do relaxation or a yoga session together or just sit together where you can feel some fresh air. Try a pretend 'spa day' – really just a chance to put up your feet, have a hand massage and remember to take it easy. Over time, the carer may initiate such times, which is healthy.

By helping your carer to establish a healthy routine for themselves, you are looking after them and doing a great kindness that will be felt far into the future. It is important that if the carer is feeling overwhelmed they should have your advance permission to transfer some or all of their tasks to someone else, without guilt or hesitation.

Times of stress

A care package for the carer is simple but important. This can be as a basic as a bag, basket or backpack that they can take everywhere with special things just for them. When I went to look after my friend Sue who had advanced leukaemia and we traipsed from hotels to hospitals in the US, my package contained:

- a book (one that I really liked, not just one I thought I ought to read)

- hand cream

- a notepad and pen for doodling and poetry

- some music with headphones

- a blanket/scarf

- some really nice herbal, caffeine-free teabags and chocolate sachets for us both

- some photos of my special people.

The scarf brightened up the darkest of corridors while I was waiting and the care package let me make a makeshift home wherever we needed to stay. Even if all that was available was a kettle, I could treat myself. More than that, it was my promise to myself to take care and be as emotionally and physically comfortable as possible, while things were temporarily tough. If you can help provide ideas for your carer's bag, you will be helping both of you.

Chronic conditions can be very taxing and you caring for your carer and them caring for you, is not like in the movies. No relationship is plain sailing and you might find that the person looking after you, whilst very loved, is changing from what you thought they'd always be. Perhaps you have very real issues that 'press your buttons', especially when you are together or alone in such proximity for a long time in unfamiliar roles.

Times of stress usually bring people closer together, but can also test even the strongest relationship! It is important for you both to have a person, friend or counsellor you can turn to, so you can talk through your fears and hopes (together or separately). This can bring confidential release and exploration of feelings.

Chapter 9

The finance questions
Health insurance and the costs you face

Dr Pippa Hawley

When you are well, the cost of maintaining your health will be part of your everyday expenses and should be covered by the money you make from working. If you become unwell, your finances are hit in two ways. If you are not yet retired, you will probably have to stop work, leading to a significant drop in income. At the same time, the costs of maintaining your health can become considerable, depending on what condition(s) you have, and where you live. Some treatments can have staggeringly high costs, which few people could afford by themselves, and that's on top of the regular costs of just remaining housed, clothed and fed.

Health care insurance

Insurance is a thorny issue. In most countries there is a combination of public insurance providing 'free' care for vital health care interventions, and private insurance picking up the cost of extra products and services not covered by the public system, the aim being to make the most efficient use of taxpayers' money. Going with an entirely private system leaves the poor very vulnerable when they get sick, and an entirely public system which covers every possible form of treatment would be so expensive that there would be no tax money left to pay for other elements of a civilized society, such as education, infrastructure or law enforcement! Despite many claims of the superiority of one system over another, most developed countries are converging to a similar blend of public and private funding.

I hope that wherever you live, you can access urgently needed treatments without becoming bankrupt. But there will be some care that will be worth paying for, with either your own money, or that of the pool of people who have shared their risk with you by investing in your common insurance policy.

Of course, it is better to be well-insured before you get sick. The insurance companies make their money essentially by gambling on your health, and insurance companies nearly always win. They hope that there will be more people who stay healthy than those who don't, and that the premiums they receive end up being a bit more than the payouts they have to make. The more money they have to call on when needed, the more they can ride out the fluctuations in those numbers. Clearly, they are successful in this, as many large organizations and financially savvy people invest in health insurance companies.

This makes health insurance sound like a rather cynical way to make a profit, but the insurance companies do fulfill the laudable purpose of reducing fear of financial ruin in the event of illness for those who buy their policies. Insurance companies also have an incentive to keep their customers healthy, which helps drive research into disease prevention, and ensures that cost-effective strategies for reducing illness (and thereby health care costs) are generally well-researched and covered by the plans. A mixed public-private model can also drive insurers to provide better care than purely private systems would, for example if payment to service providers is contingent on achieving meaningful outcomes, such as reduction in readmission rates and improved quality of life.

> *Buying insurance is definitely something which should be done with great consideration and attention to detail*

Insurance is not the enemy, despite all the bad press companies get from occasional conflict with individuals, frustrated in their efforts to claim on an ambiguously worded policy. If you look at the need to buy health insurance from a positive perspective, you get to win both ways, whatever your own personal outcome. If you end up being one of the unlucky policy holders who gets sick and needs to claim to pay your health care costs, you will 'win' by getting back more than you put in. If you end up subsidizing other people's health care rather than paying for your own, then you have had the good fortune to have your health rather than the money. When you die, you can't take your money with you! The worst-case scenario would be the 'double whammy' of having paid the premiums, but then having neither good health nor the ability to cover your costs. This is why it's important to know exactly what you are paying for. Some insurance policies which look too good to be true are just that, so if in doubt (and even if you think you have figured out the best deal) make sure to check with someone who understands the insurance industry well.

Other useful insurance

In addition to health care expense insurance, there are two other kinds of insurance you need to consider. One is life insurance, which may or may not be worth paying for, depending on your life expectancy and debts/assets. If you are already considered a high-risk client, the premiums may be very high, and the payout very low. You might be better off putting your money into a savings account to leave for your family, which could cover the expenses of your passing, or to pre-pay for the more expensive items such as a funeral and burial/cremation services.

The second is critical illness insurance. This kind of insurance is generally not very expensive. For example, I pay $350 CDN/year (US$275, £200 or 230 Euros) and the policy would pay out a lump sum which is not enormous, but could be a big help in the event that you develop a serious illness. Unlike life insurance, you get to spend this when you are still alive, and can use it for anything you want, including taking the family on holiday.

So, in summary, read the small print on any policy you are thinking of buying, and get advice from an independent insurance broker before committing. Check out all your options, and above all, NEVER lie on a health questionnaire. If you end up needing to claim, remember that the insurance company will do everything it can to avoid paying out. If you have something in your medical records which the company can use to claim that whatever condition you developed was not actually a new problem, it will.

What costs need to be covered?

Medical treatments vary hugely depending on what illness you have. Some can be very expensive, and be required on an ongoing basis for many years, for example hemodialysis for kidney failure, or long-term ventilation for respiratory failure. In contrast, bone marrow transplant is an example of a very expensive but (hopefully) one-time intervention.

These major treatments are almost invariably covered by public and private insurance. Exceptions include treatments that are so new they have not yet been approved by the insurers, for example some of the newer anti-cancer treatments. Many new drugs are developed every year, some of which turn out to be safe and effective, but some of which turn out to be neither. The process of making sure these new drugs are reasonable treatments, meaning their benefits outweigh the risks of taking them, and the potential benefit is deemed worth the price, can take time.

My insurance won't pay for a new 'wonder drug'. What can I do?

Occasionally, a drug comes along which seems so good that people want access to it when it's had just enough time to go through all the necessary testing, but not enough time for the insurers to decide if it's worth paying for or not. In these situations, if you really want to try the drug, you might have to pay for it yourself. This can cost many thousands per month. Sometimes the manufacturers make the product available on a 'compassionate release' program, in the hope that some of the people who take it will have such spectacularly good responses that the insurers will be spurred to decide to cover it.

As with insurance, be very careful what you commit to, as many new treatments turn out in the end to be no better than the old ones, and you can waste a whole lot of money. We will talk more about this in the clinical trials and alternative medicines sections.

Costing the extras

Though individually much less expensive, the 'little' things that tend not to be covered can add up and still be a major financial burden.

Some of the things you might need to spend money on include:

- medicines

- food supplements

- special equipment for your home such as ramps, chair lifts or hand rails

- mobility aids such as canes, walkers or wheelchairs

- transport to and from medical appointments

- new clothes if you change size or need to accommodate bodily add-ons such as colostomy bags or feeding tubes.

These may sound scary, but remember that they are designed to increase your independence and allow you to do the things you enjoy, at home and not in hospital. They are worth paying for, and best acquired early, so that you don't run the risk of being stuck somewhere and not able to get around comfortably. There are some pretty cool-looking mobility aids available now and the freedom to be able to go out and not worry about having to rest, or stop on a hill where there is nowhere to sit down can be liberating. Outings will be much more enjoyable if you can use whatever help is needed, to prepare and to get there, freeing you up to focus your attention and energy on making the most of the sights, company and activities.

Help and advice

Often there are benefits programs which can cover rental of equipment, such as walkers and wheelchairs. It may be difficult to find out about these programs, and the best source of information will be the social workers and nurses who should be part of your care team. If so far you have just seen a doctor, and received the news about being seriously ill, you may not yet know about all the other people who will be there for you over the course of your illness, including your recovery if things go well.

> *Often there are benefits programs that can cover rental of equipment, such as walkers and wheelchairs*

In the UK, it is the local authority's social care services who will assess your needs and see what can be provided and what you have to pay for. In Canada, all but the smallest hospitals have social workers and counsellors who you can ask to speak to. If you are an outpatient there are equivalent people who can provide the same service, once you know how to find them. Ask your doctor for a referral as soon as possible, as many programs do not reimburse retroactively. You may need approval in advance to pay for some services.

Claim your benefits

There may be other benefits to which you are entitled, giving you income support that is not tied to a particular expense. Employers may have sickness benefits designed for short-term absences from work, and disability benefits which cover longer term absences. Disability benefits can provide a higher income for you, but there are eligibility criteria you have to fulfil in order to receive them. It is a good idea to check on what you are entitled to as early as possible, so you can be sure to have collected the necessary documents and application forms in good time. A good example is the Canadian Compassionate Benefits Program. This covers up to 26 weeks of caring, which can be enormously helpful.

Some smaller employers have difficulty covering staff absences, so job security and return to work can be tricky, but many employers will do their best to accommodate staff who are carers of seriously ill relatives, even going beyond legal requirements.

Another possible way to reduce your outgoings is to claim some of the expenses against your tax bill. Even if you don't expect to be around to fill out your tax return at the end of the year yourself, your estate will still be liable for the tax. If you have had substantial expenses, you can reduce the amount you or your family have to pay when the time comes. This leaves more of your estate for those you would prefer to leave it to. So keep your receipts for everything.

Home support

Lastly, you may need to spend some money on paying people to help you manage your daily activities. Most modern health care systems have some provision for home care nursing, but the nurses aren't able to help with housekeeping like preparing meals or doing the laundry. If you can't do those things, you may be lucky and have friends or family who would like to do them for you. If not, you may be eligible for some funded 'home support', where people are paid to come and care for you. If not, or if you prefer to make your own arrangements, you can pay someone privately. There are agencies that can provide these services, or act as agents to find someone, for a fee. Some also take a sizeable percentage of the worker's pay as their commission, which makes it more expensive for you. You can save money by looking for someone privately, through informal networking amongst friends and family, or put a notice up on the board at your community centre or supermarket. Social media can be a very useful route, but always do your due diligence with background checks and references to avoid unscrupulous people who might take advantage of you. Thefts from disabled people by their paid caregivers are unfortunately not unheard of, but the vast majority of paid caregivers are kind and caring people who love their work, and the money you pay them is extremely well spent.

You may be eligible for some publicly funded 'home support', where people are paid to come and care for you

---

So, in summary, if you are reading this when well – maybe you are supporting a loved one who is sick – get yourself insured while your health is good. If you are already sick, take a close look at your policy and see what is covered and what isn't. Check out all the benefits to which you and your family might be entitled. Keep all your receipts for extra expenses or services: you never know what you might be able to claim back later.

Remember – you can't take your money with you, and if you have some savings, splashing out in order to enjoy the last phase of your life is money well spent!

Chapter 10

Nutrition, complementary and alternative treatments
What helps and what doesn't

Dr Pippa Hawley

When diagnosed with a serious illness, people's early reactions include asking, 'Why me?' The next question is frequently 'What can I do to help myself?'

In the turmoil of medical appointments, surgeries, drug therapies and complex decision-making, it can be easy to feel powerless and at the mercy of the medical system intent on curing you, or at least keeping you alive as long as possible. There may be very little that you feel you have control over. So you may start thinking about changing your diet, one of the few things you can still control.

Should I change my diet?

For some conditions, diet can be tremendously important. For example, in cases of kidney failure it is important not to eat too much potassium, while in heart failure salt is on the restricted list. Diabetics will be very familiar with the limits on carbohydrate intake, particularly refined sugars. If you have been provided with dietary recommendations by your medical team, stick to them.

For many conditions however, diet has not been shown to have any effect on the course of disease, particularly cancer. We know that being overweight increases the risk of some cancers, and eating a lot of some particular foods is associated with higher rates of some kinds of cancers. A diet high in processed meat is associated with bowel cancer; salt-preserved fish with stomach cancer. So far, science doesn't understand the mechanisms for how these are related, and there may be other factors which are more important and independent of diet that we don't yet know about.

Unfortunately, there is no evidence that changing your diet after you get cancer can make any difference to the cancer cells' growth.

Just eating sensibly, with plenty of fluid, fruits and vegetables, not too much alcohol and an occasional treat, will be doing the best for yourself that can be advised at present.

There has been some research on extremely low sugar diets, but not only is the evidence for any benefit very weak, this kind of diet is unappetizing and difficult to maintain. The unpleasantness of being deprived of anything sweet is likely to hugely outweigh any unproven potential benefit. Maybe in 10 years we will have more information and will be able to make specific dietary recommendations for diet and cancer control, but not yet.

> ***Just eating sensibly, with plenty of fluid, fruits
> and vegetables, not too much alcohol and an
> occasional treat, will be doing the best for yourself***

Complementary and alternative medicines — what's the difference?

Following on from diet, we can't ignore other things that people put in their bodies, namely complementary and alternative medicines, which are not at all the same things.

Complementary therapies, including medicines, are those which support or 'complement' conventional medical treatments. They don't conflict with treatment and they can help by making you feel good generally, for example having a massage, or by reducing the side-effects of treatments. Acupuncture, for instance, has been found to reduce nausea. Complementary therapies should not be harmful. At their worst, they might be ineffective for some people.

Alternative therapies, on the other hand, are a very different kettle of fish. These are unproven treatments which people hope might help a particular illness, most commonly cancer. They are widely touted for many other serious illnesses such as multiple sclerosis, as well as non-life-threatening conditions such as backache and sore feet.

Alternative therapies are unproven but, being sometimes based on a vaguely plausible scientific principle, they are sold as 'scientifically proven' to desperate people. They might be offered by naïve but well-meaning purveyors and they might be harmless, for example a well-known cold remedy. Or they might be marketed as part of a cynical, exploitative racket. Alternative therapies can be potentially dangerous, such as intravenous infusions or coffee enemas.

The best-case scenario is that an alternative treatment may eventually be found to be helpful, and the inventor is a true pioneer, but these stories are very rare. The worst-case scenario is that the treatment is one that has been proven to be useless in proper trials, such as angioplasty to the neck veins for multiple sclerosis. These treatments can in fact be worse than useless, having actually killed people.

The complexities of cannabis

Medicinal cannabis deserves a special mention here, as it is currently being heavily promoted as a cure for a huge variety of ailments. Actually, there is some evidence that it has considerable potential for benefit in some conditions. There are clinical trials showing possible benefit for nausea related to chemotherapy, cancer pain, muscle spasms in multiple sclerosis, psychosis in early schizophrenia and many other symptoms.

The potential with medical cannabis is also the problem. Cannabis is not a single entity. The cannabis plant produces hundreds of chemical compounds, many of which have pharmacological effects on our bodies, and the amounts of these compounds vary hugely from one product to another. As with many complex interventions, the devil is in the detail. We can't cover this topic thoroughly in this book, but it needs to be mentioned so that harm can be avoided if you are thinking about trying it.

Despite the plethora of anecdotal reports from well-meaning people who would like to believe it possible, there has not yet (as of 2018) been any good human clinical trial showing that any form of cannabis can cure cancer or any other serious illness. Maybe one day we will be using specific cannabis-derived treatments to treat diseases themselves, not just the symptoms, or to augment disease-modifying treatments (brain cancer being one promising area of research), but until the work has been done to enable us to do this safely and reliably, it is best to wait until we know more.

It cannot be said that cannabis might help but it at least it won't hurt. Some cannabinoids can have effects on the immune system, and some can cause some unpleasant effects which may not be reversible, especially psychosis from high dose THC (the main psychoactive cannabinoid) in young people.

The issue of harm from inhaling the nasty stuff that's in smoke cannot be ignored, and though it appears safer than tobacco smoke, it is still not a good idea to put toxic substances into your lungs, whether smoked or vapourized. So, if trying medicinal cannabis, use it in a non-inhaled form. An oil extract is probably the safest option if you are not getting good symptom control from conventional treatments. However, just as with any drug that has no clear dose-response relationship you should start low and go slow. Start with a low dose of a product with as close to an equal balance between THC and CBD (the main modulator of THC's psychoactive effects) that you can get, and only increase if the benefits appear to outweigh any side-effects. If it's not helping, stop and try something else.

How to approach alternative therapies

'Buyer beware' is the principle when considering any treatment not being offered in a proper medical setting.

- Check up on the credibility of the purveyor of the treatment

- Get at least one opinion on the proposed treatment from people who know what they are talking about

- Talk to your doctors

- Find other people with the same condition as you from disease-based societies and associations, and combine your information-finding resources

- If you have a rare condition, look up what known experts in your condition from reputable universities and hospitals are researching. Get help from your hospital's medical library staff

- If considering treatment offered by someone who is not a licensed physician, for example a naturopath, try to get independent references from past patients, not people who have been paid to provide internet testimonials of dubious reliability.

And finally, if you see a story on the internet about a new treatment which sounds too good to be true, it's probably just that – not true.

I'm not saying that miracles can't happen, and maybe the next thing to come along might turn out to be a new leap forward in medicine, but please be careful. I have seen too many people have false hopes dashed and taken advantage of financially. Worse, I have also seen people with curable cancers end up dying from them, because they decided to delay conventional treatment in favour of going somewhere for an unproven treatment, only to come back when their disease was advanced, and for it then to be incurable. Don't be the next victim of the snake oil salesman.

Chapter 11

Celebrate your life
Holding a living wake

Dr Pippa Hawley

A funeral is an event for your loved ones: to process their grief, and for community and family to show their love and respect for you. These are good things, but the event will only be of solace to you (the object of the funeral) if you have had some say in planning it. Though knowing that there is a nice funeral ahead may be of great value to some people, have you noticed how many obituaries say 'no funeral by request'. By whose request?

A funeral can be expensive, and for many people facing the end of their life it can seem irrelevant. So why not plan an event at which you will be alive and present? Why should your friends and family have to wait until after you are gone to show their love for you? Instead you could have an opportunity to get them all together one last time – a chance to say goodbye, thank you, and that you love them, or even to correct old wrongs and misunderstandings. It could be a really good party, at which you would actually get to be present. For the cost of a traditional funeral, a pre-mortem knees-up could be pretty fancy!

---

*Why not plan an event at which you will be
alive and present?*

If you are one of the people to whom this sounds appealing, you should consider a living wake.

Planning a living wake: some practical ideas

Decide on a theme. Your guests may be unfamiliar with the concept of a living wake, and may be unsure of what to expect. Having a clear theme will break the ice and make them feel more comfortable. Remember that this actually is all about you now, so you can pick whatever you want. If you are a musician you might want to have your old band get together again (Google Derek Miller – Penmachine, or search John Caspar-49 and holding, on YouTube). If you are a gourmet cook you might want a fabulous meal prepared exactly the way you want it. If you are a jazz aficionado you might want your favourite band to play. If you have very fond memories of time spent in the Caribbean you might like to have a poolside barbecue, with everyone asked to come appropriately dressed. The possibilities are endless.

Get the timing right. You will be familiar with the difficulties of prognostication, and if you have a living wake as soon as you learn you are ill, you may live for a long time afterwards. You might even be cured. It is a good idea to wait until you are reasonably sure that things are on a downward trend, or you could end up having to have multiple living wakes. Everyone knows of someone who 'was given three months to live' and ended up surviving and thriving for another 10 years.

On the other hand, if you leave it too late you might be too unwell to enjoy it. This is particularly important for people who face the prospect of cognitive decline, such as in cases of dementia or liver failure, where the body may live longer than clear mental functioning. If you deteriorate faster than expected, all is not lost. Your family will now have a pretty good idea what you would have wanted, so can convert the living wake plans to a funeral instead.

> *Having a clear theme will break the ice and make guests feel more comfortable*

Form a team. There will be a lot to do, and you need to preserve your energy for the event itself. Allowing people who care for you to feel useful is a gift you can give. Allocate everyone a job and have someone else fret about getting it all done in time. The process is much like a wedding, with little details making a big impact.

Pick a good venue. If you want a small number of very close friends then you might be fine having your living wake in your own or a friend/family member's home. Most people, however, find that the invitation list swells beyond the number that can be fitted into a normal house, and unless you own a mansion, or live in an apartment complex with a party room, a larger space usually becomes necessary.

Allow for breaks. Make sure that wherever you choose has a private area, preferably with a bed or sofa where you can retreat for a rest if you need it during the event. You may be unable to handle 4 to 5 straight hours of socializing, but with a 'power nap' in the middle you will be able to stay engaged until everyone goes home.

Organize your invitations. Booking a venue and the catering can be tricky if you are unsure of numbers, so it is a good idea to give people as much warning as possible. You don't want to run out of food or have to turn anyone away because of fire regulations. Nor do you want to have food wasted. To reduce the uncertainty of numbers, send out proper invitations with clear instructions to RSVP, maybe even including a stamped addressed envelope and a little card where people tick yes or no, like a wedding, just to make sure. Or you could use one of the on-line invitation sites such Evite, if all your guests are comfortable using the internet.

Be sure to state clearly how long it will last, and that the purpose of the event is to celebrate life and to say good-bye, so people can get their head round the concept before they come.

Attaching a current photo to the invitation will save people who have not seen you for a while from the shock of your looking different due to your illness, such as having lost a lot of weight, or your hair being shorter following a particular cancer treatment. Conversely, showing that you still look like you will reassure people, so that they don't worry and stay away.

Because it's a party, your guests will want to bring gifts. Suggest to them that bringing a memory or photo of time together would be much appreciated. This prevents anyone feeling uncomfortable about trying to think of something suitable.

Example: John's invitation

Time is running out. Can't say how much I have left but according to sources usually deemed reliable my days are definitely numbered — although I'd always hoped they'd be lettered instead.

Two years ago, I attended a bucket list festival and learned about living wakes. You can look it up if the concept isn't clear. If you're not doing anything on October 4th, come on over and find out how it works. Consider it an opportunity to tell me what you REALLY think about me before it's too late. I consider it an opportunity to tell you how much you've meant to me and my best friend Sharie over the years, particularly the last two decades when it was pretty much a day-to-day proposition. There are so many of you who made the struggle worthwhile and thank you for helping me stay the course.

In my usual 'traveling hopefully' frame of mind I'm calling this the First Annual JF Living Wake, so if you can't make this one, stay in touch for news of the next. The only condition for attendance is that you come empty-handed. Bring a smile, a thirst, an appetite and, if you like, a story or a song. We'll lay on some cheap beer, home-made wine, soft drinks and nibbles.

Capture it. Arrange for a photographer to record the event. This is partly so you can look back and see all the people who were there, even if you didn't get as much time to talk to everyone individually as you would have liked. It is also for your family to look back on later, as part of your legacy. Encourage people to take their own photos, especially of themselves with you.

Have a practice run. You may like to talk to your doctor about this, especially if he or she has experience with palliative care medications. Having a good night's sleep the night before may be easier to achieve with an appropriate sedative, but as sleeping pills can have side-effects, even a paradoxical effect, it is importance to know exactly what the effect will be. You may need a few tries until you perfect the timing and the dose. Being able to stay awake until late may be a challenge, and if you are going for an evening event you may benefit from a short-acting stimulant such as methylphenidate (Ritalin). Again, a couple of test evenings can allow you to refine the dose and timing so you can predict how long you will be good for.

---

*Encourage people to take their own photos,
especially of themselves with you*

Think about the activities. Ideas that might appeal to different members of your team include a guest book, speeches, slide show, menu cards, music selection, decorations/flowers and so on. Make sure to include children, even if they are quite young: allowing them to contribute to the event will be a long-lasting memory and is a gift from you to them.

Speeches and silence. If you are not comfortable with public speaking you may not want to make a speech but try to have even a short interlude where everyone is quiet together, as this gives shape to the event and gives your guests permission to acknowledge the purpose of them all being there. Talking about death and dying is a taboo topic, and though you may have wrapped your head around it already, your guests may not. Clearly putting the subject on the table will allow your guests to open up and make the most of the opportunity to talk, both with you and with each other.

On the day – relax and enjoy it! Don't worry about everything being perfect. When did you go to a wedding where everything went without a hitch? And don't you mostly remember the hitches with affection? Embrace the unexpected, and don't be shy. This is not a time to hang back and worry about what other people think. Apologize for anything you feel bad about, which most people won't even have remembered, and probably never cared about anyway. It will make you feel better at least! Be kind to people when they share their need for forgiveness with you. Try to have everyone (including you) leave with no regrets.

Afterwards. Thank people for attending, send photographs, and make sure they know that you still want to see them. You are not dead yet...

Chapter 12

Creating a legacy
Helpful ways to leave supportive, meaningful messages

Gaby Eirew

There are many things you will feel you cannot control, but you can control the emotional legacy you leave for your family and those close to you.

From 2007-2011, I interviewed more than 100 people who had been children when their parents died. The research focused on what emotional or physical legacy they received from their parents and how it affected them. This research helps us understand what people, especially children, could benefit from knowing about their parents, which might help them at the time of their parents' death and far beyond.

Generally, people were ill-prepared for death. Only a small minority had drawn up a will, few had an advanced care document and no-one had prepared something – anything – of emotional value for their children. I was shocked. The mere fact of your reading this book suggests you are actively planning to do something, which is wonderful.

This is not to negate what parents do for children and family while alive, nor how resilient people are when they have to cope with loss. No-one will take away your child's memories of time spent with you nor the crucial early years, when the parent is there and nurturing, which sets our sense of self.

Our research points to a number of ways in which you can leave a positive emotional legacy for your family, so that young (or not so young) children can enjoy enhanced memories of you. This is relevant for grandparents as well as parents: your grandchildren may be young now and relatively incurious about your life 'in the old days', but there will come a time when they will welcome knowing more about you.

As well as talking to your children now, you can prepare ways in which they will have a tangible legacy of you in the future. Find your photos and mementoes to give them and make use of technology to leave them your voice and your moving image.

If you would like to make a video recording for yourself, or those close to you, the Recordmenow Society has made a free, private app for you to record yourself on your computer or phone. See www.Recordmenow.org for more information. Importantly – if you do make a recording, ensure people know about it and how to access it.

Let them hear your voice
'I love you Emma'

Children who have lost a parent are often told how loved they were. But whilst this is kind and comforting, children yearn to hear the parent say it directly to them. This is especially so, if the parent dies when the child is very young. With all the cool devices available now, making a recording is easy to do. See the Appendix for more information on the Recordmenow app.

Technology makes recordings easy to do now and we should use this to bring the past into the present

---

Let them know that the death or illness was not their fault 'My illness is just bad luck'

What small children 'learn' from the death of a parent is not necessarily what the adults around them intend. A number of people who replied to my questionnaire said they had struggled with the feeling that they had either contributed to the death or had not helped prevent it. Explaining that you have an illness that was just bad luck would be helpful.

Let them know you want them to live on happily 'I'm very sad to die but I am delighted you will live on and can have a full life'

While your family will certainly grieve for you, it will really help your child to be told that the best way they can honour your memory is to live on and live fully. This should reassure them as they grow up.

Let them hear about life before sickness
'There was a lovely day when we went to the park and...'

For many children, it is helpful to create pictures and accounts of normal and good times, before illness struck: favourite meals, family jokes, trips to the park or the library – all the stuff of an ordinary, happy day. You can also ensure they learn about your own happy times too, including before they were born, your school and college years, wedding, holidays and so on – so that as they grow up, they will have an understanding of you as a fulfilled adult. You can also answer questions which your child will be too young to ask now but may want to know the answers to later, for instance stories of work and puberty, romance, further education, career choices and adventures.

Talk about your favourite products
'My current toiletry/candles/shaving foam brands are...'

What products do you use? What soap do you like? What makes the apartment smell so good? Some people like to honour and remember their parent by wearing the same brand of lipstick or enjoy their house having the same special smell. Unlike a tangible item, knowing your brands can mean that your child can enjoy honouring your memory while no one else might need to know.

Talk about your traditions
'On special days we like to...'

What are your beliefs? Perhaps you can talk about your or your parent's traditions, so your child can feel more connected – they may want to just know or even wish to carry on some of those traditions.

Give a sense of yourself in your work
'The work I have most enjoyed is...'
'I got my first job...'
'I liked the responsibility of...'

People generally want a broader picture of their parent and to know about their youth. They want to know how their parent chose a career, handled work-life balance, how they coped in relationships, as well as any quirks or funny habits.

Hobbies and activities
'I have really enjoyed...'

Hobbies might feel far away but remembering them is not only interesting for your family to know, it also can give you great pleasure to think about. In our research, people said they wanted to know what sports teams their parent supported so they could consider supporting them too. What music do you listen to? Where do you walk for relaxation? Maybe your child will walk that route with their partner or their own children one day.

Give them permission to love others
'I love you, our love is forever, it will never be diminished and it is fine to love others who come into your lives'

Permission and encouragement to love others, without your child feeling that in so doing, they are betraying you, is very important. Loving people going forward is particularly key when the child and family will be reliant on the care of new people in the future, such as perhaps step-parents, stepsiblings, future partners and their own children. Knowing that love is infinite and transcends dying is important.

Leave things for people, and say why
'I am leaving you this because...'

Sentimental things are precious and needn't be expensive at all. Young children are often left nothing when a parent dies. Being left something specific and to hear why – to show your

child has been specifically thought about and has something to treasure is wonderful. Ideally select something which has a story or memory attached to it; and, nothing too easily breakable! It might be a scarf you wore from the lovely day in the park recently. One young man I know, ironed, pinned and framed his mother's scarf and it hangs proud and brightly above his dining table.

Making a doll from pieces of material from favourite clothes can be very comforting to a small child, or a quilt for older children/adults. The one pictured was made from pieces of especially memorable material. Even if you aren't able to make it yourself, you can select the material and design and have someone make it for you.

Memory and Scent

The close links between our sense of smell and memory are well documented, and it was particularly interesting to hear from two women about the importance of personal items and smells.

One woman wished she knew her mum's perfume. 'I wear her scarf, but people ask questions,' she said, and she was limited in where she could wear the scarf. She felt that if she knew her mother's perfume, she could wear it any time without attracting questions. Only she would know the significance of the scent.

Another lovely lady, in a group for women with metastatic cancers, said she longed to know the name of her mother's floor cleaner. She said the smell of it triggered many happy memories for her of coming home, and that every now and again, she would enter a building, smell that fragrance and be transported back.

Olfactory memory is very strong. Your perfume, aftershave, shampoo, even floor cleaner or polish, are closely identified with by children, and it's easy for you to leave the product name.

Let them know how to grieve
'It would be fine if you grieve me by ...'

One lady I interviewed did not know how her dad wanted her to honour him so she prayed for him every day... for an hour... for decades! Not knowing what her father wanted, she was scared to stop. So, if you can give a sense of how you would like your family to grieve you or as much information on what you wish (and what you don't mind about) it would be very helpful. Some families have not been certain what burial rites their parent wanted and it has sparked family arguments. Speaking openly and candidly about your wishes lets those close to us feel they have honored you and can live on guilt free. My Dad said: 'Grieve for two years, say some prayers for me, then move on. Any more, and you're not doing it for me!' I found it characteristically funny and helpful.

Another wonderful person who had a longstanding heart condition said, 'I am not religious in the slightest – I have signed to donate my parts, give me the simplest funeral or cremation or anything, lift a beer or a cup of coffee to me every now and again and that's just fine.'

It seems that the fuller picture we can give of ourselves, and the more we can absolve our family of any guilt, the more we can help our children to digest their past, feel connected and live their life in the way we would want them to live.

Chapter 13

Near death experiences
What it's like to die, as far as we know

Dr Pippa Hawley

Having successfully resuscitated a number of people, and heard their amazing accounts, I've come to think that the actual process of dying is not to be feared. In fact, it often seems to be a very pleasant experience. People generally aren't keen to be brought back.

Despite appearing unconscious, people whose brains are shutting down are experiencing a state of heightened consciousness, full of rich meaning.

I remember one elderly retired sea captain whose heart had stopped two or three times. We got it beating and while returning to consciousness he called out 'Women and children to the boats!', clearly having had a vivid experience he was subsequently able to describe, with lots of chuckles.

There are many stories of people who have survived a near-death experience describing seeing a bright light, feeling warm and loved, and being free of pain. People dying from hypothermia report feeling warm, even to the point of taking off key pieces of clothing such as mittens. This has been reported of people caught in a storm too late in the day to be able to get down off Mount Everest.

People whose brains are shutting down are experiencing a state of heightened consciousness, full of rich meaning

---

It may be that various interpretations of these reports have, over the millennia, led to belief in some form of after-life, or heaven. Near-death experiences have been depicted in art going back almost to the birth of civilization. Some people report their life flashing before their eyes, and many report seeing deceased friends and relatives welcoming them. These beliefs cross all cultural barriers and are remarkably similar all over the world, even in groups of people who have been cut off from others, and are therefore unlikely to have picked up ideas from other cultures.

Heightened consciousness

There is good scientific evidence that these experiences are caused by massive release of neurotransmitting chemicals in the brain, with different parts of the brain generating the different experiences. For example, a study of rats in the moments after their hearts stopped beating showed a sharp increase in high frequency electrical activity, called gamma oscillations. It is thought that humans also experience the same electrical pulses in the brain shortly after cardiac death, and that these are responsible for the elevated level of consciousness described by those in whom circulation has been restored and are thus able to tell us about it. It is thought that the shutting down of the visual cortex generates the sensation of the bright light, while the shutting down of the temporal lobes creates the total memory download. This is still an area which needs much research, but there is sufficient reliable information to be able to reassure all readers that the process of dying is likely to be our last great experience, and from the sounds of it, a not-to-be-missed one. We don't know yet how different kinds of death affect the experience – for example, whether the experience is the same or not if you die under a general anesthetic. It is particularly important to remember that we don't know if drugs can affect the experience, for example in overdoses of sedative drugs, either deliberate or accidental.

So what happens then?

If you don't need to be frightened of dying, might you reasonably be frightened of what happens after that? This is where we step into the great unknown. I personally think it is unlikely that there is any experience to be enjoyed once all those electrical pulses have finally ceased and your brain cells have stopped consuming any stored energy, but the fact is that no-one knows for sure.

Even if this is the case, it doesn't mean that you as a person will immediately cease to exist, because the memory of you will live on in the consciousness of those you interacted with in life, whether family, friend, acquaintance or enemy. You also live on in the things that you created and affected during your life, such as songs, pictures, books, things you have made, the genetic legacy in your children, the personal values of your children, and others in your family if you helped raise them. Perhaps you will live on in their achievements.

> *Think about all the memories you have created in other peoples' minds and all the little things you have changed in the world around you*

Sometimes these legacies can appear small, but may endure for centuries, for example an oak tree you planted. Some people's name lives on because a place was named after them, like Hadrian's Wall or Mount Robson, but most of us don't achieve that kind of fame.

If you are wondering about what will remain of you after you have gone, think about all the memories you have created in other peoples' minds. Think of all the little things you have changed in the world around you, and if you have time, try to create some more impacts that you would still be proud of in hundreds of years' time. The people who built Stonehenge or the pyramids were not thinking short-term. If your legacy does not seem very substantial to you, then maybe you have time to do a little more to make people remember you with a smile.

Chapter 14

What happens to bodies?
The science and practicalities of after death

Dr Pippa Hawley

Having discussed what might happen to your consciousness and your legacy, we should make sure that the vessel in which you have lived your life is not forgotten on your path to whatever your afterlife looks like. From the moment that you cease to be able to use oxygen, your body's cells start to disintegrate. The brain is the most energy-consuming part of our bodies, and brain cells will start to fall apart before more stable tissues in the body. If left to nature, other tissues will follow, in a gradual series until eventually all the 'soft' tissues of our body become liquid, in a process aptly termed decomposition. All that tissue eventually makes its way into the soil or the sea and is recycled via plants and animals incorporating them into new growth.

The rigid structures we have made over the years will be left behind, manly bones and teeth. In certain conditions, inside a dry, cool place protected from predators, such as inside a pyramid, frozen into a glacier or permafrost, these bits of us can last a very long time. Little bits of tissue can persist for thousands of years in the right conditions, for example in the roots of the teeth. A 9,000 year old human skull found in a cave near the town of Cheddar in England (famed for its cheese) yielded dental tissue which was used to determine that at least one local resident in the nearby village was a descendant of that person. The skeleton of King Richard III was dug up more than 500 years after his death, when a car park in Leicester was being redeveloped. His identity was confirmed, not just by the prominent scoliosis of the spine (remember he was a famous hunchback) but also by the same techniques of tissue analysis and comparison with known descendants.

If you want someone to be able to do this in hundreds of years, there are people who will take your money and promise to cryogenically preserve you, but I for one would not be keen on that. If I died of something pretty nasty, especially at an old age, I wouldn't want to be brought back to life in that sorry state. Better to be done with that particular body and hope the carbon atoms that temporarily collaborated to make me got redistributed into worthier organic substances, like new babies, trees or earthworms.

For those of you that are happy to just have your body recycled, you have a number of choices.

Burial

You can have your body put into a coffin and then buried in a designated place. The reason for designation being required is to avoid accidental exhumation during house renovations and the like. In epidemic conditions, there were also safety concerns, with the living preferring not to catch the germ that did you in, like the plague, cholera or leprosy. You can choose what kind of container you get buried in, and other details, such as whether you are horizontal or vertical, or squished into a large pottery container as was once fashionable in some cultures.

You can have a wicker coffin, with flowers and mementoes woven into the willow, or have a wooden coffin you made yourself years before and used as a blanket chest, or stood upright as a bookcase. It could be a cardboard construction (with or without messages written on with a Sharpie by those left behind), or it could be a beautiful hardwood multi-layered work of art with solid gold handles. There are 'Coffin Clubs' in some places, for example one in New Zealand with branches in multiple cities and towns throughout the country. People join the club and learn the skills to construct bespoke containers for their or a loved one's body, or even to donate for those families who cannot afford one or want something special (www.coffinclubs.co.nz).

However, little of this will matter once it's six feet under, and unless you have gone to an awful lot of effort to get buried in a lead-lined coffin or bullet-proof sealed glass container, eventually the coffin will rot away, allowing the earthworms, beetles and other instruments of the great carbon recycling system to get in and start spreading your atoms far and wide. If this is not something you are comfortable with, then you may prefer another form of disposal. I did have one patient who after nearly an hour of trying to figure out what was worrying her, finally blurted out the question of whether or not worms could get into coffins, and had presumably been lying awake imagining this with some horror. I hope I advised her appropriately (answer above).

Burial does offer the opportunity for a substantial physical memorial, such as a headstone or even a tomb, and many people like the idea that their loved ones will have somewhere to go to visit them. On the other hand, it is the most expensive form of body disposal, both in terms of the actual funeral and in the subsequent maintenance costs. Ask yourself whether you would prefer that the money be better spent, for example on a bench for people to sit on at your favourite walk's pausing point, or a contribution to a new playground at your local park or school. Maybe even given to a charity who will use it wisely to help the living.

Cremation

Cremation is the quickest route to redistribution of your carbon, it almost all being released into the air by combustion in a large gas oven, leaving behind just some ashes which can be conveniently packaged for scattering or storage. The practice of being burnt on an open funeral pyre is limited to certain parts of the world. Though cheaper than having to have a plot of earth in which to be buried, being cremated still requires a coffin of some sort. The ashes will be a mix of what is left of you, the clothes you were wearing, and whatever your coffin was made of, including any hinges and handles, though these are usually removed by the funeral home before the ashes are packaged for collection. Most funeral homes now have 'gardens of rest' where ashes can be stored for a fee, and there can be a plaque, like a mini gravestone, in your honour. This does provide a place for people to visit should they wish to do so, but like a grave, does require long-term maintenance to remain legible many years later.

As we age in the era of amazing medical interventions, many of us will have accumulated some extra bits and pieces, such as artificial hips, lumps of acrylic cement, surgical clips and pacemakers. These extra items should be well-documented before death just in case you end up being cremated, as sometimes they can be a hazard to those providing this service. Anything with a battery (like a pacemaker) could explode, and it is usual to have these removed first if cremation is being considered. Be sure to write this clearly in any will or other advance directive, and make sure your relatives know what you have inside you, just in case. Storage will also be an issue if surviving relatives wish to keep all of their loved one's remains. My mother for example has had both knees, both hips and both shoulders replaced, and a container to hold all those bits of metal would have to be much more substantial than a little urn! Unfortunately, none of these devices can be recycled for use in another person, even if they had only just been put in.

Scattering of ashes can be restricted, and you should check the local regulations about this before planning a ceremonial scattering. For example, where I live in Vancouver there is a designated area for the scattering of ashes at sea for those who are members of the yacht clubs in the area. That being said, if done surreptitiously, or far from the prying eyes of any official, you can pretty much scatter them where you want. It's not as if anyone will ask you to collect them back up again! Many people derive considerable peace in knowing that their ashes will be scattered in a particular place, and that place can be just as much of a destination in which to mourn and remember as a gravestone or plaque on a wall, even if it is only known to those close to you.

Other options

There is a myriad of alternative funeral options now available, some ancient and some modern. A traditional Viking funeral where the body is put in a boat which is set on fire and then pushed out to sea is understandably illegal in many places, presumably because of the high risk of incomplete combustion which could lead to a nasty surprise on an early morning beach-walk, or a hazard to shipping. Being laid out on a raised platform in the American desert for the birds to come and slowly peck apart is definitely out of fashion, as are a large number of old burial practices, but fortunately there are some new ones which are much more socially acceptable, some particularly environmentally friendly.

Green funerals

A variety of containers are available in which your ashes can be buried, mixed with potting soil and a seedling of what will eventually be a tree, with special forests designed to accommodate these legacy trees. Some companies will even offer to bury you in a coffin, but upright as opposed to the usual horizontal, in order to take up less space on our crowded soil. If you think about it, especially in crowded parts of the globe with a long history of dense human occupancy, we are literally standing on the remains of our ancestors, and with the phenomenal increase in the world's population, all of whom will become bodies eventually, we have to be aware of the need to have space to put them. There are many options which can be found in the internet, and there are forms of body disposal which are tasteful and environmentally friendly, available at a whole variety of price points.

Green Burial Canada: www.greenburialcanada.ca

Green Burial Council of North America: www.greenburialcouncil.org

Natural Death Centre – Association of Natural Burial Grounds UK: www.naturaldeath.org.uk

Natural Death Care Centre Australia: www.naturaldeathcarecentre.org

Donating your body to science

Fostering science is a very worthy legacy. Trainee doctors need to be able to learn anatomy through dissecting and examining bodies 'in the flesh' so to speak, as well as looking at images and diagrams. If you would like to donate your body for this purpose you will need to contact the medical school well in advance of your anticipated demise. They will explain the process to you, and let you know the circumstances under which it might not be possible, such as if you died from an infectious disease. Donating your body to science doesn't mean it will reside in a medical school anatomy lab forever. If all goes according to plan, the medical school will take possession of your body promptly after your death; they will treat it very respectfully; and you will be returned to your loved ones some months later for disposal by a method of your choosing (and at your own cost). If you prefer not to have them deal with that you can make prior arrangements for your remains to be disposed of by cremation.

Organ donation

If you haven't already had to think about this when you got your driving licence, think about this now. You shouldn't wait until you think you might have a life-threatening illness before registering as an organ donor, as the best source of organs is from a healthy person who has been in an accident, by definition not knowing that they were about to become a potential donor. Having a non-accidental death does make it harder to use your organs, as they will not be in ideal shape, but some parts of you can still be useful even if you died of cancer, especially your corneas. The main transparent part of the cornea does not contain any cells, so they can be transplanted into people whose corneas are no longer transparent because of scarring from infection, burns or other trauma. The gift of vision can be an incredible legacy.

There is a very short window of opportunity after someone dies before the organs deteriorate irreversibly and are no good for transplant, so it is not OK to wait until the time comes before talking about it. Tell your family, write it down, tell your doctor, tattoo it across your chest, do whatever you can do to let people know if you would like to be considered as an organ donor, should you meet with an untimely end.

Chapter 15

Suicide, euthanasia and medically assisted dying.
What these words mean

Dr Pippa Hawley

This book would not be complete without mentioning suicide, euthanasia and medically assisted dying, even if just to clarify the meaning of the terms, and to explain what the current situation is regarding 'unnatural' life endings.

Suicide is a well-understood term, meaning the deliberate act by an individual of wilfully ending their own life. It is understandable that thoughts of suicide can occur to a person with a terminal illness, but suicide has huge negative consequences for those left behind.

Because assisting someone to commit suicide is illegal in most parts of the world, usually suicides happen (deliberately) in private, allowing no opportunity for anyone to try to change the person's mind. We will come to medically assisted death in a moment.

The important negatives of suicide are firstly that the people left behind are often very traumatized, and secondly that any chance of resolving the problem which was creating the wish to die is lost forever. Loved ones of victims of suicide have a higher risk of prolonged and dysfunctional grief. It is hard enough for someone to lose a loved one, without the extra burden of knowing that the person who died had rejected a life the survivor was part of. Those left behind almost inevitably feel they could and should have done something to prevent the suicide.

Once suicide starts to involve other people, it becomes a whole lot more complicated.

First some terms.

Euthanasia is the process whereby someone is deliberately killed, with the intent of stopping unrelievable suffering. This can be with or without the consent of the sick person. Euthanasia is allowed in a variety of forms in some parts of the world, such as the Netherlands, Belgium, Switzerland, Canada and some states in the US. Each jurisdiction has slightly different rules regarding how the procedure is administered, and how the person's consent is determined to be clear and genuine, without influence from someone else who might benefit from the death. Euthanasia without consent is only different from murder by the intent of the person doing it.

This is a very tricky subject as it is impossible for one person to assess another's suffering. What may be intolerable to one person may be acceptable to another, and if that person is unable to communicate, they could become the victim of well-intentioned but unwelcome termination of life. It is also possible for the most vulnerable in society to be killed for less than altruistic motives under a euthanasia umbrella. This is the 'slippery slope' commonly referred to and the main reason why euthanasia is still illegal throughout most of the world.

Medical Assistance in Dying (MAiD) is the term currently used to describe euthanasia provided by a doctor with the recipient's consent in Canada. The procedure has a number of other terms, including Physician Assisted Suicide, Medically Hastened Death, or Physician Hastened Death.

Discontinuation of life-prolonging treatment is NOT euthanasia. Studies of places where referenda have been held about whether to legalize euthanasia have shown that many people confuse these two situations. For example, in Quebec MAiD was decriminalized a year ahead of the rest of Canada because of a provincial referendum showing that a majority of voters supported it. Unfortunately, a subsequent study showed that many voters thought that discontinuation of life-prolonging treatments was the same as euthanasia. They were not voting for physicians to be able to legally kill people on their request, but for an end to what they thought was unwelcome prolongation of life, by putting suffering patients on to machines to keep them alive when they didn't want to be. This is an important reason to be very clear about this subject if your country, state or province is going through the throes of legalization.

No-one has ever been obliged to accept any medical treatment offered, unless they are not considered competent to make that decision, by reason of being a child or of having cognitive impairment, in which case the best substitute decision-maker is allowed to make that decision, all with the person's best interests as the only concern. Saying no to medical treatments is, and has always been, completely legal, whatever the reasons for your choice, and even if many would under the same circumstances not agree.

This is not the place to argue in detail the rights and wrongs of MAiD, but it is important when contemplating or discussing it to at least understand what the terms mean. If you live in the part of the world where MAiD is not legal, you may be presented with the opportunity to vote for or against it in some form in the future. Please be as informed as possible, and whatever you decide, make sure your choice is based on a clear and accurate understanding of the issues. A prerequisite should be that every citizen has access to the specialist palliative care and other physical, social, psychological and spiritual supports necessary, to ensure that people are not forced to choose MAiD when their suffering would be preventable or treatable if those supports were in place.

Chapter 16

Inspirational groups
Amazing projects to help you out and help you through

Gaby Eirew

When bad things happen, it is tempting to shut down, batten down the hatches and think that we need to be alone to cope with the onslaught. Whilst privacy and time to yourself is important, it's equally important to get support from people and to support others in return. Accessing help is a great strength and you will be rewarded with some fantastic groups out there: established, experienced, ready and able to help.

So you don't need to repeat the groundwork, look into what support exists locally that might benefit you and your family – use this like a salad bar, and take the ideas and wisdom that you need. To get you started, here in this chapter is information on a tiny sample of wonderful groups that already exist.

You might want to do an internet search of what similar groups exist near you or, if you love what they are doing, start your own group. We will have a website constantly updated with well-reviewed groups from around the world – if you know of a particularly good one, please tell us online at **www.lapofhonourbook.com**

Patient and family counselling services

Social workers and counsellors understand the challenges of cancer and other life-threatening conditions. They can provide individual, couple and family counselling as well as support groups and education programs to support you. These services are usually provided at no cost and are available to patients, families, caregivers and friends who are supporting patients. The services are available from the time of diagnosis, through treatment and often for months following the end of treatment.

Most hospitals and chronic disease management programs run a range of support groups, such as a drop-in one for women with metastatic cancers.

e.g. www.bccancer.bc.ca/our-services/centres-clinics/vancouver-centre/support-programs

The groups meet regularly to share their experience and wisdom but registration and regular attendance are not usually necessary. Being with peers means attendees develop an understanding of their condition and can swap stories of how they are grappling with living knowing their time is limited, but not having any certain timeline.

The groups let you be your uncensored self, working through and sharing your challenges and successes with others. Good groups have a rare honesty and humour that accompany a safe, supportive environment. Confidentiality and being there for each other are key, and it can feel fulfilling because you are contributing as well as benefitting. You are able to attend a session and then, crucially, leave issues there to ponder as you return to your life, with supportive stories or others' wisdom, knowing that you can attend next time to listen and share more.

The counsellor's role in these groups is less to counsel than to gently guide and facilitate, ensuring that all the participants feel safe and comfortable within the group.

Counselling support groups: emotional support along the way

A huge number of organizations offer counselling; individual, family and group and co-counselling. You can access this in person or via online forums. Some groups such as Cancerconnection.ca offer it over the phone. Most of those run by health organizations will be free or heavily subsidized.

General counselling offers a time set aside where you can check into your feelings and express how you are – from hopeless and desperate and angry or optimistic. At its base is a safe, non-judgmental space for you to reflect on how you are doing, be that how you are feeling about yourself or what role you are taking in relationships or how you are balancing the rigours of your condition. Essentially, counselling can offer you a dedicated time to slow down and think about how you are doing and what has been going on for you. Whatever feelings come up are fine. The counsellor and group can hold the emotions without judging or breaking confidence and feelings are carefully respected as valid and your own. Throughout treatment, you may be offered a range of support groups, from groups for your family, to specific groups for people with your condition.

We come to illness as complex individuals, so it is important that you select an approach to counselling that sits well with you. It should be on the theme with which you most identify and where you want to get support. You can choose whether you want to be in a general group or in a specific group, or if you need someone to call you or see you privately, where the focus corresponds directly to your concerns. Conversely, you might benefit from hearing the experiences of others with the same condition. Or you might be looking for more specific support.

> *We come to illness as complex individuals, so it is important that you select an approach to counselling that sits well with you*

There can be many reasons why counselling for yourself or your family can be helpful. It's very normal and healthy that when a family is dealing with life threatening conditions, old psychological problems can intensify or reappear when you thought they were a thing of the past. Obsessiveness can get exacerbated under pressure; and children can seem to regress with thumb-sucking, bedwetting and nightmares, even before they are told about the issues. As one boy aged 11, asked about how his mother's sickness and depression affected him said: 'I didn't understand what was happening. No-one had said anything but I knew the mood of everything – I could feel the tone had changed and that really worried me.'

Depression may loom, old cycles or previously suppressed fears may surface, so it is important to look at what is a simply a question of weathering the change and what you need to talk about as a family or get help for. Just because your body is struggling with a condition does not mean you should ignore your feelings or state of mind. There are some fantastic doctors and counsellors available to support you emotionally. Your family doctor as well as your specialist should be able to guide you.

If you are considering more general counselling, you may wish to select a particular approach that has appealed to you or helped you in the past. Cognitive behavioral therapy (CBT) for example gets very good reviews from people dealing with anxiety and depression and can help quite quickly with day to day concerns. You may benefit from talking to your family doctor or specialist about your feelings; they want to support you as a whole person and they can reassure you if some of the feelings may be linked to your condition, treatment or medication.

> *Just because your body is struggling with a condition does not mean you should ignore your feelings and state of mind*

You and your family are grappling with a lot and your emotional wellbeing is a key part of that. If you are part of a trial, you might not find others going through the same treatment or placebo-medication frustrations, but you can benefit from the support of the group in many other ways. It needs to work for you.

The basics – questions to ask

Check where and when the groups take place, so you can cope with the logistics of regular or drop in attendance. Can you attend online if you cannot attend in person? Can you rest there if you get tired?

Ensure that the counsellor is trained and insured and confirm that all sessions are completely confidential. Is it the kind of counselling with which you feel comfortable, or might be able to get comfortable? Ask away and shop around just as you might with any important decision. You may feel desperate for help but do take time and advice – support needs to be a fit with you.

Children's support groups

Different members of the family may need support either as a unit or separately. There are some wonderful groups and online resources for children whose parents are coping with illness.

Children may feel that they don't want to rock the boat by bringing up difficult feelings at certain times at home, or because they may equate 'being good' or 'helping dad' with subduing their own feelings. It is not just adults who fear if they start opening up they will never be put back together again. One young woman, aged 17, said: 'I am scared that if one tear comes, it will let the others come and I will drown in my tears, so I just can't start.'

Having a place to kick back, say how frightened you feel and still be accepted as a kid with others who 'get you' is key. Some places will even have simultaneous sessions for the children and an adult or carer, so both get support and then meet for a closing session. Simply hearing other children able to talk and hear about the full gamut of emotions in relation to their parent's sickness can be very helpful to the child who, through youth or shock, cannot yet put everything into words. Also play therapy or support groups for children of unwell patients can sometimes feed into supportive grief groups where the children will already be familiar with the facilitator and some of the participants. Children's groups and grief groups are often run by or attached to hospices, or specialist health facilities.

A regular children's play therapy group might take a format such as:

- Check in. Going around the group, each child says how their week was. To make it less raw, this may be put in the form of a metaphor, so instead of saying, 'I feel so angry', the children may be invited to give a weather update and say: 'Today I feel so stormy, with trees flying all over the place and dogs lifted up, but I think the clouds are softening a bit'.

- Next children might do an exercise on a theme – like making a collage or song of all the different feelings they may have, or creating poems about change.

- Afterwards they may have a snack or runaround and have general chat. But the talking is with the knowledge that everyone is there because a parent is very sick or dying, so the talk stays deep and focuses on how the children are sincerely feeling.

- Perhaps the sessions end with a ritual song or lighting a candle and saying the family member's name, acting as a poignant closing ceremony till the following week.

Bucket List Festivals

Among the difficulties people face on hearing a bad prognosis is remembering what the doctor said and not knowing what to do next. Bucket List Festivals give people a whole day opportunity to ask questions, reduce the fear, connect and find out more about living with life-limiting conditions and end of life issues; many of the issues central to this book. From talks on travelling while sick, to doctors relaying how to access care, and raffles for balloon rides, Bucket List Festivals have a wonderful quality of honesty and information. The setting is upbeat, usually at a hotel, supported by hospice volunteers. Everyone has a comfortable seat at a table throughout the day and there are ample opportunities to swap stories, ask questions, connect with the speakers and with each other, as well as to rest during the day.

As an example, see the videos from the 2017 Vancouver Festival on www.bucketlistfestivalvancouver.org

Other helpful ideas

Lotsahelpinghands.com – a computerized system for co-ordinating your volunteer help

Lotsahelpinghands.com is a 'care calendar' website which anyone can make use of. It is a wonderful system allowing people to co-ordinate the many offers of help from family, friends or even local volunteers. Instead of trying to write your own programme, or hundreds of emails, Lotsahelpinghands lets one key person, 'the co-ordinator,' co-ordinate multiple roles for which you might need help. This allows you to reach out to get hospital drives, food and medical deliveries, shopping, gardening, house cleaning, house sitting – all without directly asking. This is particularly useful if you do not have a large network nearby or if as a family, you are coping with a long degenerative or immobilizing condition. Many family and friends will want to help – they just need to be told what you'd like and Lotsahelpinghands makes it much easier for everyone.

www.LotsahelpingHands.com

Cancer support groups

The Callanish Society (Callanish.org), based in Vancouver, is an example of a non-profit organization that offers counselling and wonderful short retreats for people dealing with life-limiting conditions. Callanish are famous for their safe environment, warmth and food as well as their intimate groups of support. They use song and art and are very well reviewed. Callanish offers counselling, meditation, support groups, healing circles and other ceremonies 'deeply rooted in the fundamentals of what it means to be human.'

The UK's Macmillan Cancer Support has a directory of similar groups on its website (macmillan.org.uk).

Down under, the Cancer Society New Zealand www.cancernz.org.nz is a good starting point for finding support groups and in Australia the health service website www.canceraustralia.gov.au has a database of groups.

The American Society of Clinical Oncology has an excellent website with an extensive directory of groups (www.cancer.net/coping-with-cancer/finding-support-and-information/general-cancer-groups)

Death Cafés – Talking about death

Death Cafés have sprouted all over the world, with 1500 in the UK alone and 300 in Australia. Their activities range from online chatting forums to large-scale New York 5th Avenue dinner parties. They are simply a time and venue set aside to discuss death, as widely or personally as you like. They tend to inspire people from researchers to philosophers to ethicists and religious eccentrics, but they can be a good place for you to send friends who want to start listening to ideas and reflections on death as a concept. They are not a good idea for people who are actually unwell already. If you have a friend who wants to talk about death in general, encourage them to link up with a local Death Café! www.deathcafe.com

Soulumination
– Photographing near the end of life

The Seattle-based organization Soulumination goes into hospitals, hospices and homes to photograph people near the end of their lives, for themselves and their loved ones. Their Adult Legacy program photographs people who have children under 18 and who have terminal conditions. The photographs are taken by one of over 40 professional trained and sensitive photographers and 120 community volunteers, who attend quickly if necessary so a free photographic legacy is left. The photographers are sensitive about light and sound and take as good a picture as they can, given the constraints in each setting. The photographs are loving gifts to enable the family to look at, remember, and celebrate the person. www.soulumination.org

Threshold Choir – bedside singing when a person is near death

Sometimes, words are not enough and when people are feeling weak or vulnerable, song and tune may comfort like nothing else. I asked to experience a trial session of the Threshold Choir and was deeply moved by the beauty of the surround-sound and choir's sensitivity.

The choir was founded by Kate Munger, who remembered the extraordinary 'meaning and bliss' she felt when a Girl Scout singing round the camp fire. In 1990, Kate visited a friend who was terminally ill with AIDS. She recalls that after helping with the housework, she was terrified and had no idea what to do next to give support. So, she did what she most liked to do when she was afraid, and sang. Kate found that this comforted both herself and her dear friend.

Kate has an unusual recruitment approach, saying she is interested in hearing from people who 'feel the shiver' when they first hear about the Threshold Choir. Today, there are more than 100 chapters singing to people facing sickness, death or grief, in Canada, the US, Australia, New Zealand, the UK and the Netherlands. Gentle melodic songs and tunes are chosen, to 'soothe, comfort, uplift and bring peace' for individuals and their families in hospitals, homes and hospices. Their services are free and they sing usually for about 15 minutes in groups of 2-4, so they can sing in three parts or harmonies. www.thresholdchoir.org

Grief Walks – Walking in nature with others to process grief

A large number of towns and cities offer outdoor Grief Walks. You may wish to put your carer in contact with them as a kind gesture for their future. Most grief walks are free or heavily subsidized. See an example: www.griefwalk.ca

Good Funeral Guide – Information and considerations on funerals

Funerals tend to worry people, which can mean that they then might not make plans. This passes on an even bigger worry to those who have to guess their wishes at the very time they are grieving.

The www.goodfuneralguide.co.uk website is committed to being a signpost to information and guidance: giving information on goods and services available, getting debate going about a full range of funerals and how they can be appropriate and personal. They have a blog on secular funerals and celebrate and identify those organizations carrying out best practice, as well as holding accountable those which do not perform well. They list everything from tombstones and ashes to dove releases, having a home burial and planning the ceremony party in advance.

All this is offered in plain English, up-to-date and without any religious bias. They set out a fear-free, matter of fact, smorgasbord of ideas for you to consider in what you wish for in your funeral and how you want it communicated to those close to you. You can also call or email them for support.

Camp Kerry

Camp Kerry in British Columbia is only one of many

camps which support individuals and families coping with life-threatening illness grief and loss with counselling retreats and support groups. Their family retreats are particularly well established.
Campkerrysociety.org

This is just a taster of what is out there. We are not advertising any particular services, but have chosen a few examples of different resources just to give you ides of what sort of things to look for where you live. Tap into what is useful for you and your family, and do please tell us exactly what you think; send us your reviews to our website **www.lapofhonourbook.com**

Appendix

Recordmenow
– how to use the app

The Recordmenow app is an easy, free and private way to video-record your messages for the people you love.

It is private, free of charge and uses any smart phone, tablet or computer with an incorporated camera. Recordmenow Society owns the app and the not-for-profit organization manages it.

Decide if you wish to record your video messages on:
PC – download from Recordmenow.org
Mac – download from Recordmenow.org
iPhone – available from the App store

You may need to accept the prompts to go through the security wall and accept the terms and conditions to receive the download. Put the icon of Recordmenow in your tool bar of your phone or computer, if it does not happen automatically, so you can easily access it.

You will be asked for a name for your file. If you are making multiple recordings for different people, you might name them for the recipients, for example 'Mum's Memories for Suzy and family' and another 'Memories for Pauline'. Or you can give a general name such as 'Derek's memories: 2019-with love' if the recording is for multiple people.

When ready, open and scroll through the categories and select what you feel you wish to focus on. There is no right or wrong; select what you feel in the mood for. You will then see a list of possible questions; answer the ones you want. If you find this overwhelming, the most important questions have asterisks, so perhaps focus on those, or you might try answering a few questions with someone close asking or answering the questions alongside you.

You can click on each question and press the i for information button to find out why research suggested this question, then go back if you don't want to answer it. Or, press the 'Ready to Record' or red circle button when you want to record yourself. Usually the red button will flash to show you the recording is successfully happening. Press the red button again if you want to stop the recording – you may wish to press the play arrow to watch what is already recorded. You can do this any number of times.

At any time, you can pause, stop or change the category. The information you have recorded will automatically save unless you delete it (which you can do with the delete or trash icon buttons). Start as soon as you can but pace yourself so it feels comfortable.

If you want to personalize any of the questions, which is a really good idea, you can use the - or + buttons to edit questions or make up your own questions. These will automatically store for you for later. If you feel unsure about technical aspects, ask a friend to assist in uploading, moving or storing the questions for you, without opening or listening to your answers.

Please make sure you tell someone close to you that you are doing the recording and where and how to find it. You might wish to leave the memory stick with your lawyer, or your next of kin. You may wish to give them your password to your phone or laptop, if it is suitable. If you prefer not to, you can store the memories as you record them or email them on to the people directly, with instructions on whether you wish them to view the recordings now or wait for later – ideally, write a note giving permission for them to use it in a private or public capacity too. If you use memory sticks, consider using a permanent marker pen to write on the outside so it is easily identified and hard to lose.

Some people like to record answers and then watch themselves played back, telling their own story. One family watched the videos in hospital, near the end of life, when the dad was more tired and much less vocal. They felt it was a lovely way of honouring his life, listening to his stories while they sat round watching and it gave a springboard to more questions and reflections.

Many people find the idea of leaving a legacy important, so we've tried to pre-empt and dispel any of your worries.

What do I do if....
'I want to do it later'

Please start now or soon! It may feel harder in the future and once you start, you will have begun your legacy; most people who have used it, say they enjoy reminiscing. The app saves as you go, so you can simply add a question or two each day.

'It feels overwhelming'

Select one question from one category that you feel you would like to do. Choose the question you most feel like answering; ignore the others. Only the ones you answer will appear in the final recording. Do this every day if you can. Most people quite enjoy it as it brings back good memories. We used to think that remembering good times in difficult times is stressful, but we now believe that recalling happier times can give us significant solace and support.

'I look awful'

Your loved ones will enjoy seeing you no matter how you feel you look. You are beautiful and they will likely get much comfort from just seeing you and hearing your voice. It will also be a wonderful trigger to many other good memories for you and them. (The way my Dad moves on one video answer brought back a wave of very happy memories for me and let me trust my memories of him.)

'I find it tiring'

Work out when you might have most energy. Perhaps ask your doctor what timing they suggest in relation to your medication. Do as many or as few questions as you like each time. The app will record everything and what you don't like, you can delete later.

'No one cares'

I bet they do; and anyway, you will have fun doing it and reminiscing just for you. Some people have even made recordings for grandchildren not born yet or children who were adopted, in case they return and want to know more. One lady relayed that she used the app to explain how to care for her garden, and another person said when to drink the wines in her carefully collected cellar! 'Drink this when I die, drink this when you get the job, drink this when Dani gets a partner, and don't put this in mulled wine!'

'I have some other things I want to say'

That is great; use the + sign and add a heading then record away. If you like, ask a close friend or relative to help personalize the questions so they are relevant to you. They may sneak in some particularly funny, poignant or important ones. One young lady wished to know what names her dad might like for grandchildren. Another asked for a song to be sung.

'I am a private person'

That is fine – it is a private app and no one will see it unless you give it to them.

'I get upset'

That is OK. This is a challenging new time and it may well prompt feelings of wanting to talk or connect with people – a friend or a counsellor, or even an estranged person you want to get back in touch with. Take it as healthy that you are experiencing and aware of these emotions and try to set up whatever connections you feel that you need. Leaving an emotional supportive legacy is a true gift.

For extra support on using the app, you can contact gaby@recordmenow.org

HELPFUL PULL OUT CHART: *Contacts – sample care list*

In addition, to friends' and family details, have a list of the normal and their out of hours numbers for:

Name	Tel #	Out of hours
Your Home Care Nurse		
Doctor		
Neighbour		
Dentist		
Respite team		
Counsellor		
Spiritual advisor		
Dog walker		
Garden help		
Lawyer		
Local store delivery		
Your local 24-hour pharmacy		
Collect children from school		
Taxi		
Ambulance		
Others:		

TIMETABLE OF POSSIBLE HELPERS

You might want to timetable on-call friends and family to be of support.
A simple timetable will show you at what time friends tend to be available.

	Monday	Tuesday	Wednesday	Thursday	Friday	Saturday	Sunday
am							
pm							
evening							
night							

Notes:

Notes:

Notes:

Notes:

Made in the USA
Middletown, DE
13 March 2019